LIVING WITH
GOD'S COURAGE

Jesus Calling® Bible Study Series

JESUS CALLING BIBLE STUDY SERIES

LIVING WITH GOD'S COURAGE

EIGHT SESSIONS

with Karen Lee-Thorp

THOMAS NELSON
Since 1798

Published in Nashville, Tennessee, by Nelson Books, an imprint of Thomas Nelson. Nelson Books and Thomas Nelson are registered trademarks of HarperCollins Christian Publishing, Inc.

All Scripture quotations, unless otherwise indicated, are taken from The Holy Bible, New International Version®, NIV®. Copyright © 1973, 1978, 1984, 2011 by Biblica, Inc.® Used by permission. All rights reserved worldwide.

Scripture quotations marked ESV are taken from *The Holy Bible, English Standard Version*, copyright © 2001 by Crossway Bibles, a division of Good News Publishers. Used by permission. All rights reserved.

Scripture quotations marked NKJV are taken from the *New King James Version*. Copyright © 1982 by Thomas Nelson. Used by permission. All rights reserved.

ISBN 978-0-310-08368-9

First Printing November 2016 / Printed in the United States of America

CONTENTS

INTRODUCTION

Sometimes our busy and difficult lives give us the impression that God is silent. We cry out to Him, but our feelings tell us that He isn't answering our prayers. In this, our feelings are incorrect. God hears the prayers of His children and speaks right into the situations in which we find ourselves. The trouble is that our lives are often too hectic, our minds too distracted, for us to take in what He offers.

This *Jesus Calling* Bible study is designed to help individuals and groups meditate on the words of Scripture and hear them not just as words said to people long ago but as words said to us today in the here and now. The goal is to help the heart open up and respond to what the mind reads—to encounter the living God as He speaks through the Scriptures. The writer to the Hebrews tells us:

In the past God spoke to our ancestors through the prophets at many times and in various ways, but in these last days he has spoken to us by his Son, whom he appointed heir of all things, and through whom also he made the universe. The Son is the radiance of God's glory and the exact representation of his being, sustaining all things by his powerful word.

—HEBREWS 1:1–3

God has spoken to us through His Son, Jesus Christ. The New Testament gives us the chance to walk with Jesus, see what He does, and hear Him speak into the sometimes confusing situations in which we find ourselves. The Old Testament tells us the story of how God prepared a people to be the family of Jesus, and in the experiences of those men and women we find our own lives mirrored.

THE GOAL OF THIS SERIES

The *Jesus Calling Bible Study Series* offers you a chance to lay down your cares, enter God's Presence, and hear Him speak through His Word. You will get to spend some time silently studying a passage of Scripture, and then, if you're meeting with a group, openly sharing your insights and hearing what others discovered. You'll also get to discuss excerpts from the *Jesus Calling* devotional that relate to the themes of the Bible passages. In this way, you will learn how to better make space in your life for the Spirit of God to speak to you through the Word of God and the people of God.

THE FLOW OF EACH SESSION

Each session of this study guide contains the following elements:

- CONSIDER IT. The two questions in this opening section serve as an icebreaker to help you start thinking about the theme of the session, connecting it to your own past or present experience and allowing you to get to know the others in your group more deeply. If you've had a busy day and your mind is full of distractions, these questions can help you better focus.

- EXPERIENCE IT. Here you will find two readings from *Jesus Calling* along with some questions for reflection. This is your chance to talk with others about the biblical principles found within the *Jesus Calling* devotions. Can you relate to what each reading describes? What insights from God's Word does it illuminate? What does it motivate you to do? This section will assist you in applying these biblical principles to your everyday habits.

- STUDY IT. Next you'll explore a Scripture passage connected to the session topic and the readings from *Jesus Calling.* You will not only analyze these Bible passages but also pray through them in ways designed to engage your heart and your head. You'll first talk with your group about what the verse or verses means and then spend several minutes in silence, letting God speak into your life through His Word.

- LIVE IT. Finally, you will find five days' worth of suggested Scripture passages that you can pray through on your own during the week. Suggested questions for additional study and reflection are provided.

FOR LEADERS

If you are leading a group through this study guide, please see the Leader's Notes at the end of the guide. You'll find background on the design of the study as well as suggested answers for some of the study questions.

COURAGE TO OBEY THE LORD'S INSTRUCTIONS

CONSIDER IT

God's instructions for our lives often take us out of our comfort zone and into a place where we need to rely on Him to get the job done. We follow Him not just into the green pastures but also through the valley of the shadow of death (see Psalm 23). Fear is a natural response to such times of risk, and it is only through courage that we can press forward and obey God even when there are good reasons to be afraid. In this first session, we'll put ourselves into the shoes of the Israelites in the Bible and look at the risk God asked them to take to secure the Promised Land. We will look at the people's fears and reactions and see that the courage to obey God is firmly founded in the promises of God.

1. *What thoughts and images come to mind when you hear the word "courage"? What sorts of individuals or professions do you think of?*

2. *Do you relate to the idea of needing courage in your life? Why or why not?*

EXPERIENCE IT

"Do not be afraid, for I am with you. Hear Me saying *Peace, be still* to your restless heart. No matter what happens, *I will never leave you or forsake you.* Let this assurance soak into your mind and heart, until you overflow with Joy. *Though the earth give way and the mountains fall into the heart of the sea*, you need not fear!

"The media relentlessly proclaim bad news: for breakfast, lunch, and dinner. A steady diet of their fare will sicken you. Instead of focusing on fickle, ever-changing news broadcasts, tune in to the living Word—the One who is always the same. Let Scripture saturate your mind and heart, and you will walk steadily along the path of Life. Even though you don't know what will happen tomorrow, you can be absolutely sure of your ultimate destination. *I hold you by your right hand, and afterward I will take you into Glory.*"

—FROM *JESUS CALLING*, APRIL 20

3. *Jesus calmed a storm by saying, "Peace, be still" (Mark 4:39 NKJV), to the wind and waves. How easy is it for you to be at peace in your heart? What helps you? What gets in the way?*

4. *How does tuning into the Word of God give us courage in the midst of the media's constant barrage of bad news?*

"Be willing to go out on a limb with Me. If that is where I am leading you, it is the safest place to be. Your desire to live a risk-free life is a form of unbelief. Your longing to live close to Me is at odds with your attempts to minimize risk. You are approaching a crossroads in your journey. In order to follow Me wholeheartedly, you must relinquish your tendency to play it safe.

"Let Me lead you step by step through this day. If your primary focus is on Me, you can walk along perilous paths without being afraid. Eventually, you will learn to relax and enjoy the adventure of our journey together. As long as you stay close to Me, My sovereign Presence protects you wherever you go."

—FROM *JESUS CALLING*, DECEMBER 9

5. *When has Jesus asked you to "go out on a limb" with Him? What was the result?*

6. *Do you tend to play it safe, or are you fairly comfortable with taking risks? What motivates you to take risks that line up with God's leading?*

STUDY IT

Read aloud the following passage from Deuteronomy 31:1–8. God had called Moses to confront Pharaoh and lead the Israelites out of slavery in Egypt. Moses had gone out on a limb and obeyed God, but when the people refused to conquer the Promised Land, he was forced to wander with them for forty years in the desert. The events in this passage take place toward the end of this time, when the people were finally ready to enter the Promised Land. God had appointed Joshua to lead the invasion, and Moses, nearing the end of his life, was offering them some final words of instruction.

[1] Then Moses went out and spoke these words to all Israel: [2] "I am now a hundred and twenty years old and I am no longer able to lead you. The LORD has said to me, 'You shall not cross the Jordan.' [3] The LORD your God himself will cross over ahead of you. He will destroy these nations before you, and you will take possession of their land. Joshua also will cross over ahead of you, as the LORD said. [4] And the LORD will do to them what he did to Sihon and Og, the kings of the Amorites, whom he destroyed along with their land. [5] The LORD will deliver them to you, and you must do to them all that I have commanded you. [6] Be strong and courageous. Do not be afraid or terrified because of them, for the LORD your God goes with you; he will never leave you nor forsake you."

[7] Then Moses summoned Joshua and said to him in the presence of all Israel, "Be strong and courageous, for you must go with this people into the land that the LORD swore to their ancestors to give them, and you must divide it among them as their inheritance. [8] The LORD himself goes before you and will be with you; he will never leave you nor forsake you. Do not be afraid; do not be discouraged."

7. *What did the Israelites need courage to do? What did Joshua need courage to do?*

8. *On what promises was their courage based? Do those promises apply to you? Explain.*

9. *What do you need courage to do? If you are a believer, how can God's promises help you in this situation?*

10. *Take two minutes of silence to reread the passage, looking for a sentence, phrase, or even one word that stands out as something Jesus may want you to focus on in your life. If you're meeting with a group, the leader will keep track of time. At the end of two minutes, you may share your word or phrase with the group if you wish.*

11. *Read the passage aloud again. Take another two minutes of silence, prayerfully considering what response God might want you to make to what you have read in His Word. If you're meeting with a group, the leader will again keep track of time. At the end of two minutes, you may share what came to you in the silence if you wish.*

12. *What was it like for you to sit in silence with the passage? Did soaking it in like this help you understand it better than before?*

13. *If you're meeting with a group, how can the members pray for you? If you're using this study on your own, what would you like to say to God right now?*

LIVE IT

At the end of each session you'll find suggested Scripture readings for spending time alone with God during five days of the coming week. This week, the theme of each reading will focus on how you can be courageous when God asks you to take a leap of faith with Him. Read each passage slowly, pausing to think about what is being said. Rather than approaching this as an assignment to complete, think of it as an opportunity to meet with the One who loves you most. Use any of the questions that are helpful.

Day 1

Read Deuteronomy 31:23. What does God tell Joshua to do?

What promise does God give him?

In Deuteronomy 31:6–7, Moses had instructed the people to "be strong and courageous" because the Lord promised to be with them. Why do you think God repeats this instruction and promise to Joshua in verse 23?

Does the repetition help you? If so, how?

Tell God anything that stands in the way of your being strong and courageous, and seek His help in overcoming those obstacles.

Day 2

Read Psalm 89:1–4. What reasons for courage does the psalmist offer?

_____

_____

_____

_____

How would you define faithfulness?

_____

_____

_____

Why is faithfulness a quality of God that you should value highly?

_____

_____

_____

_____

_____

When have you experienced God's faithfulness toward you personally?

Use these verses as a springboard for your own prayer to God, praising Him for who He is and what He does.

Day 3

Read Psalm 89:5–8. The psalmist speaks of God's faithfulness two more times in this passage. Why do you think the biblical writer repeatedly spoke of this characteristic of God?

The psalmist also says there is no one like God anywhere (see verse 6). Why is that a reason for every son or daughter of God to have courage?

When you think of God as mighty, how does that affect you?

When you think of God as being "surrounded" by faithfulness, how does that affect you?

Choose one of the qualities of God depicted in these verses and praise Him for it.

Day 4

Read Psalm 89:9–13. How does the psalmist depict God's power?

What impact do these words have on your own courage?

_____

_____

_____

_____

Where do you see God's power at work in the world around you and in your own life?

_____

_____

_____

_____

Where do you long to see more of God's power?

_____

_____

_____

_____

Turn your longing into a prayer that leaves room for God to work in surprising ways and not according to your agenda or timetable.

Day 5

Read Psalm 89:14–18. Why are you grateful for God's righteousness and justice?

When have you been aware of God's Presence with you this week?

How will you rely on God as your strength today?

What gives you courage right now?

_____

_____

_____

Today, thank God for His commitment to justice, for His Presence, and for His Strength.

COURAGE TO
CONFRONT A
STRONGER FORCE

CONSIDER IT

Sometimes we look at a challenge before us and know we lack the strength to do what God is asking of us. The challenge is big . . . and we are small. We see this happen often to the men and women in the Bible as well. In fact, it happens so frequently that it seems to be a pattern God delights in! He does this so it will be obvious that He deserves the credit if something good happens, not us. In this session, we'll look closely at a familiar Bible story to see what courage we can gain from the Lord to face the challenges that are before us.

1. *When have you encountered a challenge that felt too big for you, either in your childhood or adulthood?*

2. *Did you meet the challenge? Did you try but not quite make it? Did you back away and not try? Explain.*

EXPERIENCE IT

"Trust Me and don't be afraid, for I am your Strength and Song. Think what it means to have Me as your Strength. I spoke the universe into existence;

My Power is absolutely unlimited! Human weakness, consecrated to Me, is like a magnet, drawing My Power into your neediness. However, fear can block the flow of My Strength into you. Instead of trying to fight your fears, concentrate on trusting Me. When you relate to Me in confident trust, there is no limit to how much I can strengthen you.

"Remember that I am also your Song. I want you to share My Joy, living in conscious awareness of My Presence. Rejoice as we journey together toward heaven; join Me in singing My Song."

—FROM *JESUS CALLING*, MARCH 21

3. *Have you ever experienced fear blocking the flow of God's Strength into you? Why do you suppose fear can do this in a person?*

4. *Why does it work better to concentrate on trusting in God rather than trying to fight your fears?*

"I am a mighty God. *Nothing is too difficult for Me.* I have chosen to use weak ones like you to accomplish My purposes. Your weakness is designed to open you up to My Power. Therefore, do not fear your limitations or measure the day's demands against your strength. What I require of you is to stay connected to Me, living in trusting dependence on My limitless resources. When you face unexpected demands, there is no need to panic. Remember that *I am with you*. Talk with Me, and listen while I talk you through each challenging situation.

"I am not a careless God. When I allow difficulties to come into your life, I equip you fully to handle them. Relax in My Presence, trusting in My Strength."

—FROM *JESUS CALLING*, MAY 14

5. *What should you do when faced with difficulties? What shouldn't you do? What does the Bible say God will do for His children?*

6. *Describe your usual response to difficulties. How is it like and unlike what has been discussed so far?*

STUDY IT

Read aloud the following passage from 1 Samuel 17:1–50. As you read, note that the Israelites were at war with the Philistines for control of the Promised Land. Saul was Israel's king, but he wasn't always obedient to God. The Philistine named Goliath was more than nine feet tall, and he was calling the Israelites to engage in a custom in which the overall battle was decided in a contest between each side's strongest warrior. The story of young David and the intimidating Goliath is long but vividly told, so you might want to take turns reading aloud in the group.

[1] Now the Philistines gathered their forces for war and assembled at Sokoh in Judah. . . . [3] The Philistines occupied one hill and the Israelites another, with the valley between them.

[4] A champion named Goliath, who was from Gath, came out of the Philistine camp. His height was six cubits and a span. [5] He had a bronze helmet on his head and wore a coat of scale armor of bronze weighing five thousand shekels; [6] on his legs he wore bronze greaves, and a bronze javelin was slung on his back. [7] His spear shaft was like a weaver's rod, and its iron point weighed six hundred shekels. His shield bearer went ahead of him.

[8] Goliath stood and shouted to the ranks of Israel, "Why do you come out and line up for battle? Am I not a Philistine, and are you not the servants of Saul? Choose a man and have him come down to me. [9] If he is able to fight and kill me, we will become your subjects; but if I overcome him and kill him, you will become our subjects and serve us." [10] Then the Philistine said, "This day I defy the armies of Israel! Give me a man and let us fight each other." [11] On hearing the Philistine's words, Saul and all the Israelites were dismayed and terrified.

[12] Now David was the son of an Ephrathite named Jesse, who was from Bethlehem in Judah. Jesse had eight sons, and in Saul's time he was very old. [13] Jesse's three oldest sons had followed Saul to the war: The firstborn was Eliab; the second, Abinadab; and the third, Shammah. [14] David was the youngest. The three oldest followed Saul, [15] but David went back and forth from Saul to tend his father's sheep at Bethlehem.

[16] For forty days the Philistine came forward every morning and evening and took his stand.

[17] Now Jesse said to his son David, "Take this ephah of roasted grain and these ten loaves of bread for your brothers and hurry to their camp. [18] Take along these ten cheeses to the commander of their unit. See how your brothers are and bring back some assurance from them. [19] They are

with Saul and all the men of Israel in the Valley of Elah, fighting against the Philistines."

²⁰ Early in the morning David left the flock in the care of a shepherd, loaded up and set out, as Jesse had directed. He reached the camp as the army was going out to its battle positions, shouting the war cry. ²¹ Israel and the Philistines were drawing up their lines facing each other. ²² David left his things with the keeper of supplies, ran to the battle lines and asked his brothers how they were. ²³ As he was talking with them, Goliath, the Philistine champion from Gath, stepped out from his lines and shouted his usual defiance, and David heard it. ²⁴ Whenever the Israelites saw the man, they all fled from him in great fear.

²⁵ Now the Israelites had been saying, "Do you see how this man keeps coming out? He comes out to defy Israel. The king will give great wealth to the man who kills him. He will also give him his daughter in marriage and will exempt his family from taxes in Israel."

²⁶ David asked the men standing near him, "What will be done for the man who kills this Philistine and removes this disgrace from Israel? Who is this uncircumcised Philistine that he should defy the armies of the living God?"

²⁷ They repeated to him what they had been saying and told him, "This is what will be done for the man who kills him."

²⁸ When Eliab, David's oldest brother, heard him speaking with the men, he burned with anger at him and asked, "Why have you come down here? And with whom did you leave those few sheep in the wilderness? I know how conceited you are and how wicked your heart is; you came down only to watch the battle."

²⁹ "Now what have I done?" said David. "Can't I even speak?" ³⁰ He then turned away to someone else and brought up the same matter, and the men answered him as before. ³¹ What David said was overheard and reported to Saul, and Saul sent for him.

³² David said to Saul, "Let no one lose heart on account of this Philistine; your servant will go and fight him."

³³ Saul replied, "You are not able to go out against this Philistine and

fight him; you are only a young man, and he has been a warrior from his youth."

[34] But David said to Saul, "Your servant has been keeping his father's sheep. When a lion or a bear came and carried off a sheep from the flock, [35] I went after it, struck it and rescued the sheep from its mouth. When it turned on me, I seized it by its hair, struck it and killed it. [36] Your servant has killed both the lion and the bear; this uncircumcised Philistine will be like one of them, because he has defied the armies of the living God. [37] The LORD who rescued me from the paw of the lion and the paw of the bear will rescue me from the hand of this Philistine."

Saul said to David, "Go, and the LORD be with you."

[38] Then Saul dressed David in his own tunic. He put a coat of armor on him and a bronze helmet on his head. [39] David fastened on his sword over the tunic and tried walking around, because he was not used to them.

"I cannot go in these," he said to Saul, "because I am not used to them." So he took them off. [40] Then he took his staff in his hand, chose five smooth stones from the stream, put them in the pouch of his shepherd's bag and, with his sling in his hand, approached the Philistine.

[41] Meanwhile, the Philistine, with his shield bearer in front of him, kept coming closer to David. [42] He looked David over and saw that he was little more than a boy, glowing with health and handsome, and he despised him. [43] He said to David, "Am I a dog, that you come at me with sticks?" And the Philistine cursed David by his gods. [44] "Come here," he said, "and I'll give your flesh to the birds and the wild animals!"

[45] David said to the Philistine, "You come against me with sword and spear and javelin, but I come against you in the name of the LORD Almighty, the God of the armies of Israel, whom you have defied. [46] This day the LORD will deliver you into my hands, and I'll strike you down and cut off your head. This very day I will give the carcasses of the Philistine army to the birds and the wild animals, and the whole world will know that there is a God in Israel. [47] All those gathered here will know that it is not by sword or spear that the LORD saves; for the battle is the LORD's, and he will give all of you into our hands."

⁴⁸ As the Philistine moved closer to attack him, David ran quickly toward the battle line to meet him. ⁴⁹ Reaching into his bag and taking out a stone, he slung it and struck the Philistine on the forehead. The stone sank into his forehead, and he fell facedown on the ground.

⁵⁰ So David triumphed over the Philistine with a sling and a stone; without a sword in his hand he struck down the Philistine and killed him.

7. *What gave Goliath his courage in battle? In whom or what was he apparently trusting?*

8. *What gave David courage in this fight? What does he say about his sources of courage in verses 34–37 and 45–47?*

9. *Why does God often choose to work through an "ordinary" person— someone who isn't obviously the strongest one in an area of endeavor (see verse 47)?*

10. *The story of David and Goliath has inspired many generations of Christians with courage. Why is this the case? What is it about this story that is so motivating?*

11. *Take two minutes of silence to reread 1 Samuel 17:45–47, looking for a sentence, phrase, or even one word that stands out as something Jesus may want you to focus on in your life. If you're meeting with a group, the leader will keep track of time. At the end of two minutes, you may share your word or phrase with the group if you wish.*

12. *Read verses 45–47 aloud again. Take another two minutes of silence, prayerfully considering what response God might want you to make to what you have read in His Word. If you're meeting with a group, the leader will again keep track of time. At the end of two minutes, you may share what came to you in the silence if you wish.*

13. *If you're meeting with a group, how can the members pray for you? If you're using this study on your own, what would you like to say to God right now?*

LIVE IT

The theme of this week's daily Scripture readings is having courage in the midst of weakness. Read each passage slowly, pausing to think about what is being said. Rather than approaching this as an assignment to complete, think of it as an opportunity to meet with the One who loves you most. Use any of the questions that are helpful.

Day 1

Read 2 Corinthians 12:6–10. We don't know the nature of Paul's thorn in the flesh, but what does he say here about its function in his life?

What does God mean when He says to Paul that His power is "made perfect" in his weakness?

_____

_____

_____

_____

What weaknesses do you have? Can you imagine boasting about them? Why or why not?

_____

_____

_____

_____

How are your weaknesses bringing glory to God?

_____

_____

_____

_____

Take a few minutes today to think about the weaknesses in your life and actually *thank God* for the ways they are furthering your faith.

Day 2

Read Luke 1:26–38. In verse 37, the angel tells Mary, "Nothing will be impossible with God" (ESV), or according to another translation, "No word from God will ever fail" (NIV). How does this story illustrate the angel's words?

What is the seemingly impossible thing that God is promising to Mary in this story?

What are some of the things that God has promised to you?

What will you be brave enough to do today, knowing that nothing is impossible for God?

Praise God for the many times He does seemingly impossible things!

Day 3

Read Isaiah 12:2–6. What reason does Isaiah offer in this passage for not being afraid?

What reasons does he offer for having joy?

How does joy contribute to courage?

_____

_____

_____

_____

Why is it important to "make known among the nations" what God has done (verse 4)?

_____

_____

_____

_____

Pray this passage aloud to God and let it foster joy—and courage—within you.

Day 4

Read 2 Timothy 1:5–8. What do you think it means to "fan into flame the gift of God" (verse 6)? How is this related to courage?

_____

_____

_____

Why did Paul remind Timothy that God didn't give him a spirit of fear (see verse 7)?

Where could Timothy get the courage to join Paul in suffering for the gospel?

Would you be willing to suffer for the gospel? Why or why not?

Today, ask God to give you courage through His Spirit for whatever tasks He has put before you.

Day 5

Read Proverbs 28:1. The righteous aren't always, every minute, as bold as a lion, but this proverb states what tends to be the case. What is it about true righteousness that inclines a person to become bold?

What does the writer mean when he states, "the wicked flee though no one pursues"?

_____

_____

_____

What is it about wickedness that can lead to cowardice?

_____

_____

_____

In what ways does this proverb encourage you? Explain.

_____

_____

_____

Thank God for giving you every reason to be bold as you strive to live a life that honors Him.

COURAGE TO SAY NO TO FALSE GODS

CONSIDER IT

We know that God is jealous for our love (see Exodus 20:5), and He hates it when our loyalty goes to anything—people, possessions, pleasures—other than Him. Sometimes, though, there's an earthly price to be paid for not putting a person or a job first. We risk losing that person's approval or risk losing that job. At those times, it takes real courage to say, "No, God comes first. God's agenda for my life comes first. I will not bow down to this just because someone has the power to make my life miserable if I don't." In this session, we're going to look at the story of three young men who made this very choice.

1. *Have you ever known someone who acted like he or she wanted to be put in the place of God? If so, how did that person make this desire known?*

2. *How did you respond to that person? What did it cost you to put God first?*

EXPERIENCE IT

"*Your needs and My riches* are a perfect fit. I never meant for you to be self-sufficient. Instead, I designed you to need Me not only for daily bread but also for fulfillment of deep yearnings. I carefully crafted your longings and feelings of incompleteness, to point you to Me. Therefore, do not try to bury or deny these feelings. Beware also of trying to pacify these longings with lesser gods: people, possessions, power.

"Come to Me in all your neediness, with defenses down and with desire to be blessed. As you spend time in My Presence, your deepest longings are fulfilled. Rejoice in your neediness, which enables you to find intimate completion in Me."

—FROM *JESUS CALLING*, DECEMBER 8

3. *Are you aware of feeling incomplete? If so, how do you typically deal with that feeling? If not, what things in your life make you feel complete?*

4. *How easy is it for you to go to God with all your neediness? What helps you do that? What gets in the way?*

"I want you to be all Mine. I am weaning you from other dependencies. Your security rests in Me alone—not in other people, not in circumstances. Depending only on Me may feel like walking on a tightrope, but there is a safety net underneath: *the everlasting arms*. So don't be afraid of falling. Instead, look ahead to Me. I am always before you, beckoning you on—one step at a time. *Neither height nor depth, nor anything else in all creation, can separate you from My loving Presence."*

—From *Jesus Calling*, January 21

5. *What are some of the things you tend to depend on other than God? How can you eliminate any of these unhealthy dependencies in your life?*

_____

_____

_____

6. *Why does depending on God require courage?*

_____

_____

_____

STUDY IT

Read aloud the following passage from Daniel 3:1–23. As you read, note that God had previously allowed King Nebuchadnezzar of Babylon to conquer His chosen nation, Judah, and take the Jews into captivity. Among the captives was a group of well-born Jewish young men whom Nebuchadnezzar educated in Babylon and assigned to work in the empire's bureaucracy. Three of these young men were Shadrach, Meshach, and Abednego. They faced continual challenges to remain faithful to God while serving in a foreign government that expected them to worship pagan gods. One incident is described in this passage.

¹ King Nebuchadnezzar made an image of gold, sixty cubits high and six cubits wide, and set it up on the plain of Dura in the province of Babylon. ² He then summoned the satraps, prefects, governors, advisers, treasurers, judges, magistrates and all the other provincial officials to come to the dedication of the image he had set up. ³ So the satraps, prefects, governors, advisers, treasurers, judges, magistrates and all the other provincial officials assembled for the dedication of the image that King Nebuchadnezzar had set up, and they stood before it.

⁴ Then the herald loudly proclaimed, "Nations and peoples of every language, this is what you are commanded to do: ⁵ As soon as you hear the sound of the horn, flute, zither, lyre, harp, pipe and all kinds of music, you must fall down and worship the image of gold that King Nebuchadnezzar has set up. ⁶ Whoever does not fall down and worship will immediately be thrown into a blazing furnace."

⁷ Therefore, as soon as they heard the sound of the horn, flute, zither, lyre, harp and all kinds of music, all the nations and peoples of every language fell down and worshiped the image of gold that King Nebuchadnezzar had set up.

⁸ At this time some astrologers came forward and denounced the Jews. ⁹ They said to King Nebuchadnezzar, "May the king live forever! ¹⁰ Your Majesty has issued a decree that everyone who hears the sound of the horn, flute, zither, lyre, harp, pipe and all kinds of music must fall down and worship the image of gold, ¹¹ and that whoever does not fall down and worship will be thrown into a blazing furnace. ¹² But there are some Jews whom you have set over the affairs of the province of Babylon—Shadrach, Meshach and Abednego—who pay no attention to you, Your Majesty. They neither serve your gods nor worship the image of gold you have set up."

¹³ Furious with rage, Nebuchadnezzar summoned Shadrach, Meshach and Abednego. So these men were brought before the king, ¹⁴ and Nebuchadnezzar said to them, "Is it true, Shadrach, Meshach and Abednego, that you do not serve my gods or worship the image of gold I have set up? ¹⁵ Now when you hear the sound of the horn, flute, zither,

lyre, harp, pipe and all kinds of music, if you are ready to fall down and worship the image I made, very good. But if you do not worship it, you will be thrown immediately into a blazing furnace. Then what god will be able to rescue you from my hand?"

[16] Shadrach, Meshach and Abednego replied to him, "King Nebuchadnezzar, we do not need to defend ourselves before you in this matter. [17] If we are thrown into the blazing furnace, the God we serve is able to deliver us from it, and he will deliver us from Your Majesty's hand. [18] But even if he does not, we want you to know, Your Majesty, that we will not serve your gods or worship the image of gold you have set up."

[19] Then Nebuchadnezzar was furious with Shadrach, Meshach and Abednego, and his attitude toward them changed. He ordered the furnace heated seven times hotter than usual [20] and commanded some of the strongest soldiers in his army to tie up Shadrach, Meshach and Abednego and throw them into the blazing furnace. [21] So these men, wearing their robes, trousers, turbans and other clothes, were bound and thrown into the blazing furnace. [22] The king's command was so urgent and the furnace so hot that the flames of the fire killed the soldiers who took up Shadrach, Meshach and Abednego, [23] and these three men, firmly tied, fell into the blazing furnace.

7. *How did Shadrach, Meshach, and Abednego demonstrate courage in this passage?*

8. *Why did it matter to God what Shadrach, Meshach, and Abednego chose to do in this situation? Why couldn't they just go through the motions of falling down before the golden image while secretly worshiping God in their hearts?*

9. *Look closely at what the three young men said to the king: "King Nebuchadnezzar, we do not need to defend ourselves before you in this matter. If we are thrown into the blazing furnace, the God we serve is able to deliver us from it, and he will deliver us from Your Majesty's hand. But even if he does not, we want you to know, Your Majesty, that we will not serve your gods or worship the image of gold you have set up" (verses 16–18). What did they affirm about God?*

10. *This story has a happy ending (see Daniel 3:24–30), but the three young men were prepared for it not to end this way. Even today when God's people are persecuted for their faith, they face the very real possibility of tragedy. Why is it important to have courage even when we don't know what the outcome of our choices will be?*

11. *Take two minutes of silence to reread Daniel 3:16–18, looking for a sentence, phrase, or even one word that stands out as something Jesus may want you to focus on in your life. If you're meeting with a group, the leader will keep track of time. At the end of two minutes, you may share your word or phrase with the group if you wish.*

12. *Read verses 16–18 aloud again. Take another two minutes of silence, prayerfully considering what response God might want you to make to what you have read in His Word. If you're meeting with a group, the leader will again keep track of time. At the end of two minutes, you may share what came to you in the silence if you wish.*

13. *If you're meeting with a group, how can the members pray for you? If you're using this study on your own, what would you like to say to God right now?*

LIVE IT

For this week's daily Scripture readings, you will look at a longer passage, broken into smaller portions, in which Jesus exhorts His followers to go out on a mission with courage. Read each group of verses slowly, pausing to think about what is being said. Rather than approaching this as an assignment to complete, think of it as an opportunity to meet with the One who loves you most. Use any of the questions that are helpful.

Day 1

Read Matthew 10:16–20. What does it mean to be a sheep among wolves? Why would Jesus ever ask you to put yourself in such a position?

How can a person be as shrewd as a snake and as innocent as a dove at the same time?

Why didn't Jesus' followers need to plan ahead of time what they would say when they were arrested and interrogated?

Can you imagine having the courage to face this situation yourself? What would help you?

Offer yourself to God in prayer right now, expressing your willingness to be sent out as a shrewd yet innocent witness.

Day 2

Read Matthew 10:21–23. What situation is Jesus describing in these verses?

What does Jesus say His followers can expect in this world? How do you respond emotionally to Jesus' words?

What would help a person have courage in this situation?

This kind of conflict and persecution is happening to Christians in other countries today. How can you support them?

Intercede for persecuted believers around the world, asking God to provide the courage to face their situations shrewdly and innocently.

Day 3

Read Matthew 10:24–25. The Pharisees had claimed that Jesus was deriving His power from Beelzebul, which is another name for Satan (see Luke 11:15). What point is Jesus making about this in these verses?

Have you ever been insulted because of your faith? If so, how did you respond?

Should you treat it as normal if you are insulted for being a Christian? Why or why not?

How would the way you are treated because of your faith affect the way you deal with people who don't like you? Is it a bad sign if **nobody** *is against you? Why or why not?*

Talk with God about the things people in the world don't like about Christians. Ask Him to give you the courage to graciously stand up for your beliefs.

Day 4

Read Matthew 10:26–31. When Jesus says, "There is nothing concealed that will not be disclosed" (verse 26), He is referring to the fact that the truth of the gospel will always be revealed in the end. How should this give Christ-followers the courage to proclaim His message?

What do you think of the statement, "Do not be afraid of those who kill the body but cannot kill the soul"? Does it ever feel as if others have power to kill your soul? How does it encourage you to know they really cannot if you have given your life to Christ?

What does Jesus say you should fear? How does this make you bolder in standing for Him?

What do Jesus' words about the sparrows say about the way God sees you? In what ways does this give you courage?

Today, thank God for valuing you as much as He does, and ask Him to reassure you that He is always with you so that you may be braver.

Day 5

Read Matthew 10:32–39. How do Jesus' words in verses 32–33 parallel what happened with the three young men in Daniel 3?

What does it mean to acknowledge God before others? How do you do this?

*In what sense did Jesus **not** come to bring peace? How can you have peace inside you anyway?*

What does Jesus mean when He says, "Whoever finds their life will lose it, and whoever loses their life for my sake will find it" (verse 39)? What are some of the ways that people often struggle fruitlessly to save their own lives?

Seek the Lord's help in giving you the courage this week to acknowledge Jesus publicly.

COURAGE TO
WITHSTAND
OTHERS' ENVY

CONSIDER IT

Envy is a corrosive attitude in which an individual not only covets what someone else has but also resents that person for having it. The feeling can even extend so far as to wish harm on the one who possesses the coveted item or trait. Because envy is common, it will often show its face where you least expect it. For example, you may think *no one* would ever envy you, but the truth is, the more you grow in godliness, the more likely it is that malicious people will look at your good qualities and want something bad to happen to you. This is what the prophet Daniel experienced. In this session, we will examine his courage in the face of this destructive vice.

1. *What opportunities for demonstrating courage have you had in the past few weeks?*

2. *Have you noticed yourself stepping out in faith more than you did prior to this study? In what ways?*

Experience It

"If you learn to trust Me—really trust Me—with your whole being, then nothing can separate you from My Peace. Everything you endure can be put to good use by allowing it to train you in trusting Me. This is how you foil the works of evil, growing in grace through the very adversity that was meant to harm you. Joseph was a prime example of this divine reversal, declaring to his brothers: '*You meant evil against me, but God meant it for good.*'

"Do not fear what this day, or any day, may bring your way. Concentrate on trusting Me and on doing what needs to be done. Relax in My sovereignty, remembering that I go before you, as well as with you, into each day. *Fear no evil*, for I can bring good out of every situation you will ever encounter."

—From *Jesus Calling*, May 7

3. *For believers in Christ, to "grow in grace" means to develop and mature in their relationship with God (see 2 Peter 3:18). In what ways has adversity helped you grow in this way? How has adversity affected you for good or for ill?*

4. *How is courage related to trust?*

"Follow Me one step at a time. That is all I require of you. In fact, that is the only way to move through this space/time world. You see huge mountains looming, and you start wondering how you're going to scale those heights. Meanwhile, because you're not looking where you're going, you stumble on the easy path where I am leading you now. As I help you get back on your feet, you tell Me how worried you are about the cliffs up ahead. But you don't know what will happen today, much less tomorrow. Our path may take an abrupt turn, leading you away from those mountains. There may be an easier way up the mountains than is visible from this distance. If I do lead you up the cliffs, I will equip you thoroughly for that strenuous climb. *I will even give My angels charge over you, to preserve you in all your ways.*

"Keep your mind on the present journey, enjoying My Presence. *Walk by faith, not by sight,* trusting Me to open up the way before you."

—FROM *JESUS CALLING*, FEBRUARY 1

5. *What do you think it means to follow Jesus "one step at a time"?*

6. *What are you facing today that requires courage to follow Jesus one step at a time?*

STUDY IT

Read aloud the following passage from Daniel 6:1–24. As you read, note that this story takes place late in Daniel's life. By this point, the Medes and Persians had conquered the Babylonian Empire you read about in session 3, and men like Daniel who were bureaucrats in Babylon now worked for the Medo-Persian government. Darius was the king of this new empire.

[1] It pleased Darius to appoint 120 satraps to rule throughout the kingdom, [2] with three administrators over them, one of whom was Daniel. The satraps were made accountable to them so that the king might not suffer loss. [3] Now Daniel so distinguished himself among the administrators and the satraps by his exceptional qualities that the king planned to set him over the whole kingdom. [4] At this, the administrators and the satraps tried to find grounds for charges against Daniel in his conduct of government affairs, but they were unable to do so. They could find no corruption in him, because he was trustworthy and neither corrupt nor negligent. [5] Finally these men said, "We will never find any basis for charges against this man Daniel unless it has something to do with the law of his God."

[6] So these administrators and satraps went as a group to the king and said: "May King Darius live forever! [7] The royal administrators, prefects, satraps, advisers and governors have all agreed that the king should issue an edict and enforce the decree that anyone who prays to any god or human being during the next thirty days, except to you, Your Majesty, shall be thrown into the lions' den. [8] Now, Your Majesty, issue the decree and put it in writing so that it cannot be altered—in accordance with the law of the Medes and Persians, which cannot be repealed." [9] So King Darius put the decree in writing.

[10] Now when Daniel learned that the decree had been published, he went home to his upstairs room where the windows opened toward Jerusalem. Three times a day he got down on his knees and prayed,

giving thanks to his God, just as he had done before. [11] Then these men went as a group and found Daniel praying and asking God for help. [12] So they went to the king and spoke to him about his royal decree: "Did you not publish a decree that during the next thirty days anyone who prays to any god or human being except to you, Your Majesty, would be thrown into the lions' den?"

The king answered, "The decree stands—in accordance with the law of the Medes and Persians, which cannot be repealed."

[13] Then they said to the king, "Daniel, who is one of the exiles from Judah, pays no attention to you, Your Majesty, or to the decree you put in writing. He still prays three times a day." [14] When the king heard this, he was greatly distressed; he was determined to rescue Daniel and made every effort until sundown to save him.

[15] Then the men went as a group to King Darius and said to him, "Remember, Your Majesty, that according to the law of the Medes and Persians no decree or edict that the king issues can be changed."

[16] So the king gave the order, and they brought Daniel and threw him into the lions' den. The king said to Daniel, "May your God, whom you serve continually, rescue you!"

[17] A stone was brought and placed over the mouth of the den, and the king sealed it with his own signet ring and with the rings of his nobles, so that Daniel's situation might not be changed. [18] Then the king returned to his palace and spent the night without eating and without any entertainment being brought to him. And he could not sleep.

[19] At the first light of dawn, the king got up and hurried to the lions' den. [20] When he came near the den, he called to Daniel in an anguished voice, "Daniel, servant of the living God, has your God, whom you serve continually, been able to rescue you from the lions?"

[21] Daniel answered, "May the king live forever! [22] My God sent his angel, and he shut the mouths of the lions. They have not hurt me, because I was found innocent in his sight. Nor have I ever done any wrong before you, Your Majesty."

[23] The king was overjoyed and gave orders to lift Daniel out of the

den. And when Daniel was lifted from the den, no wound was found on him, because he had trusted in his God.

²⁴ At the king's command, the men who had falsely accused Daniel were brought in and thrown into the lions' den, along with their wives and children. And before they reached the floor of the den, the lions overpowered them and crushed all their bones.

7. *How is this story like the one about the three young men in Daniel 3? How is it different?*

8. *Why did Daniel's fellow officials want to find a way to make charges against him?*

9. *Have you ever been the target of someone's hostility or bullying? If so, how did you respond? How do you wish you had responded?*

10. *What lawful alternatives did Daniel have that would have spared his life? Why didn't he just stop his private worship for the thirty days?*

11. *Take two minutes of silence to reread Daniel 6:10–14, looking for a sentence, phrase, or even one word that stands out as something Jesus may want you to focus on in your life. If you're meeting with a group, the leader will keep track of time. At the end of two minutes, you may share your word or phrase with the group if you wish.*

12. *Read verses 10–14 aloud again. Take another two minutes of silence, prayerfully considering what response God might want you to make to what you have read in His Word. If you're meeting with a group, the leader will again keep track of time. At the end of two minutes, you may share what came to you in the silence if you wish.*

13. *If you're meeting with a group, how can the members pray for you? If you're using this study on your own, what would you like to say to God right now?*

LIVE IT

The theme of this week's daily Scripture readings is having courage in the midst of bullying, envy, and hostility from others. Read each passage slowly, pausing to think about what is being said. Rather than approaching this as an assignment to complete, think of it as an opportunity to meet with the One who loves you most. Use any of the questions that are helpful.

Day 1

Read Psalm 27:1–3. What reasons for fear does the psalmist mention in these verses? What reasons for courage does he mention?

What does it mean to say that God is your "light"? What does it mean to call Him your "stronghold" (verse 1)?

What enemies do you have that want to bring you down?

How can you use the encouragement of these verses to stand firm in faith?

Let these verses be a springboard to your own prayer of praise and confidence today.

Day 2

Read Psalm 27:4–6. What did it mean in the psalmist's time to live in the house of God (see verse 4)? How can you do something similar today?

How can you behold "the beauty of the LORD" (verse 4)?

What reasons for courage does the psalmist offer in verse 5? How can you experience these?

Why does the psalmist sing (see verse 6)? What reasons do you have for singing to the Lord?

Sing or speak your own prayer of joy to the Lord for all that He has done for you.

Day 3

Read Psalm 27:7–10. What does it mean to seek God's face? How can you do that today?

What do you want to cry aloud to God? How can you be confident that He will hear you?

How is the Lord more to be trusted than earthly parents (see verse 10)?

When you were a child, did your parents give you security and courage, or was your home life unstable? How can you know that your Father in heaven will never forsake you as His child?

Take a few moments to thank God for being a perfect, caring, and loving heavenly Father. Thank Him for never forsaking you and for being the Savior.

Day 4

Read Psalm 27:11–14. What reasons for fear does the psalmist express in these verses?

What confidence does the psalmist speak of in verse 13? What difference does this promise make to followers of Christ in their current situation?

What does waiting for the Lord (see verse 14) have to do with taking courage? Why is it courageous to wait for God?

What are you waiting for God to do in your life?

Today, pray a prayer in which you express your willingness to wait courageously for the Lord.

Day 5

Read Deuteronomy 33:26–29. What reasons for courage do these verses offer?

What picture do you get when you try to imagine God's "everlasting arms" (verse 27)?

What does it mean to "dwell secure in a land of grain and new wine" (verse 28)? How does God provide this type of security in your life?

As a believer, in what ways has the Lord proven to be your shield and sword (see verse 29)?

_____

_____

_____

Conclude by praising God for being the things this passage says He is for you: One who "rides across the heavens" to help you (verse 26), One who holds you up with "everlasting arms" (verse 27), and One who is "your shield and helper" (verse 29).

COURAGE TO
PROTEST AGAINST
WRONG

CONSIDER IT

In Ecclesiastes 3:1, we read, "There is a time for everything, and a season for every activity under the heavens." There is a time to plant and a time to uproot, a time to weep and a time to laugh, a time to keep and a time to throw away (see verses 2–4, 6). The author also tells us there is "a time to be silent and a time to speak" (verse 7). In some cases, the correct action is to be still and accept what is happening. At other times, the correct course is to risk speaking out, especially when it involves someone being wronged. In this session, you'll explore the story of a woman who had the courage to speak up in a dangerous situation. Hopefully, her story will inspire you to take whatever step of faith God is calling you to take . . . even if it means speaking truth to those in power.

1. *When you were a child, were you the kind who spoke up and asked for what you needed (maybe even in a demanding way), or did you tend to more passively accept whatever happened? Explain.*

2. *What are some ways you would like to be bolder when it comes to standing up for others?*

Experience It

"Walk by faith, not by sight. As you take steps of faith, depending on Me, I will show you how much I can do for you. If you live your life too safely, you will never know the thrill of seeing Me work through you. When I gave you My Spirit, I empowered you to live beyond your natural ability and strength. That's why it is so wrong to measure your energy level against the challenges ahead of you. The issue is not your strength but Mine, which is limitless. By walking close to Me, you can accomplish My purposes in My strength."

—From *Jesus Calling*, March 11

3. *What does it mean to walk by faith, not by sight?*

_____

_____

_____

4. *Why don't we need to live our lives too safely? Do you tend to live too safely? What is the evidence?*

_____

_____

_____

"Expect to encounter adversity in your life, remembering that you live in a deeply fallen world. Stop trying to find a way that circumvents difficulties. The main problem with an easy life is that it masks your need for Me. When you became a Christian, I infused My very Life into you, empowering you to live on a supernatural plane by depending on Me.

"Anticipate coming face to face with impossibilities: situations totally beyond your ability to handle. This awareness of your inadequacy is not something you should try to evade. It is precisely where I want you—the best place to encounter Me in *My Glory and Power*. When you see armies of problems marching toward you, cry out to Me! Allow Me to fight for you. Watch Me working on your behalf, as you *rest in the shadow of My Almighty Presence*."

—FROM *JESUS CALLING*, AUGUST 18

5. *Have you ever come face to face with a situation totally beyond your ability to handle? If so, what happened? Was God there to bring you through it?*

_____

_____

_____

_____

6. *Do you crave an easy life? What's the evidence?*

_____

_____

_____

STUDY IT

Read aloud the following passage from Esther 4:4–5:5 and 7:1–6. Note that this story takes place during the time when many Jews were still living in exile. A Persian king named Xerxes wanted a new queen, so he sent his soldiers into the towns and villages to find beautiful young women for his harem. The king spent one night with each of these women until he found the one he wanted as his queen: a Jewish woman named Esther.

Esther had a pampered position, but she was not allowed to leave the king's harem even to visit her uncle, Mordecai—and he was not allowed to visit her. She was also not free to see the king whenever she liked. If he wanted to see her, he would send for her. But one day Mordecai learned that one of the king's officials, Haman, had received permission from the king to kill all the Jews in the empire on a certain day. To alert Esther to the situation, Mordecai went to the palace gate, wailing and wearing sackcloth as a sign of mourning. The story picks up from there.

4:4 When Esther's eunuchs and female attendants came and told her about Mordecai, she was in great distress. She sent clothes for him to put on instead of his sackcloth, but he would not accept them. [5] Then Esther summoned Hathak, one of the king's eunuchs assigned to attend her, and ordered him to find out what was troubling Mordecai and why.

[6] So Hathak went out to Mordecai in the open square of the city in front of the king's gate. [7] Mordecai told him everything that had happened to him, including the exact amount of money Haman had promised to pay into the royal treasury for the destruction of the Jews. [8] He also gave him a copy of the text of the edict for their annihilation, which had been published in Susa, to show to Esther and explain it to her, and he told him to instruct her to go into the king's presence to beg for mercy and plead with him for her people.

[9] Hathak went back and reported to Esther what Mordecai had said. [10] Then she instructed him to say to Mordecai, [11] "All the king's officials and the people of the royal provinces know that for any man or woman who approaches the king in the inner court without being summoned the king has but one law: that they be put to death unless the king extends the gold scepter to them and spares their lives. But thirty days have passed since I was called to go to the king."

[12] When Esther's words were reported to Mordecai, [13] he sent back this answer: "Do not think that because you are in the king's house you alone of all the Jews will escape. [14] For if you remain silent at this time, relief and deliverance for the Jews will arise from another place, but you and your father's family will perish. And who knows but that you have come to your royal position for such a time as this?"

[15] Then Esther sent this reply to Mordecai: [16] "Go, gather together all the Jews who are in Susa, and fast for me. Do not eat or drink for three days, night or day. I and my attendants will fast as you do. When this is done, I will go to the king, even though it is against the law. And if I perish, I perish."

[17] So Mordecai went away and carried out all of Esther's instructions.

[5:1] On the third day Esther put on her royal robes and stood in the inner court of the palace, in front of the king's hall. The king was sitting on his royal throne in the hall, facing the entrance. [2] When he saw Queen Esther standing in the court, he was pleased with her and held out to her the gold scepter that was in his hand. So Esther approached and touched the tip of the scepter.

[3] Then the king asked, "What is it, Queen Esther? What is your request? Even up to half the kingdom, it will be given you."

[4] "If it pleases the king," replied Esther, "let the king, together with Haman, come today to a banquet I have prepared for him."

[5] "Bring Haman at once," the king said, "so that we may do what Esther asks." . . .

[7:1] So the king and Haman went to Queen Esther's banquet, [2] and as they were drinking wine on the second day, the king again asked, "Queen Esther, what is your petition? It will be given you. What is your request? Even up to half the kingdom, it will be granted."

[3] Then Queen Esther answered, "If I have found favor with you, Your Majesty, and if it pleases you, grant me my life—this is my petition. And spare my people—this is my request. [4] For I and my people have been sold to be destroyed, killed and annihilated. If we had merely been

sold as male and female slaves, I would have kept quiet, because no such distress would justify disturbing the king."

[5] King Xerxes asked Queen Esther, "Who is he? Where is he—the man who has dared to do such a thing?"

[6] Esther said, "An adversary and enemy! This vile Haman!"

7. *What did Esther do that was courageous? Why did it take courage to do what she did?*

8. *What risk did Esther face if she was too afraid to take action?*

9. *This story never mentions God, or even prayer, yet where is He in this account?*

10. *Esther was in just the right place at just the right time to speak up on behalf of the Jews. What are you in just the right place for when it comes to helping others?*

11. *Take two minutes of silence to reread Esther 4:12–16, looking for a sentence, phrase, or even one word that stands out as something Jesus may want you to focus on in your life. If you're meeting with a group, the leader will keep track of time. At the end of two minutes, you may share your word or phrase with the group if you wish.*

12. *Read verses 12–16 aloud again. Take another two minutes of silence, prayerfully considering what response God might want you to make to what you have read in His Word. If you're meeting with a group, the leader will again keep track of time. At the end of two minutes, you may share what came to you in the silence if you wish.*

13. *If you're meeting with a group, how can the members pray for you? If you're using this study on your own, what would you like to say to God right now?*

LIVE IT

The theme of this week's daily Scripture readings is having courage to stand up for the needs of others. Read each passage slowly, pausing to think about what is being said. Rather than approaching this as an assignment to complete, think of it as an opportunity to meet with the One who loves you most. Use any of the questions that are helpful.

Day 1

Read Mark 5:21–24. Why did Jairus need courage in this situation? What risk was he taking?

Read verses 35–36. What further need for courage did Jairus have?

Now read verses 37–43. What was the outcome of this situation?

What do you think would have happened if Jairus had allowed fear to take over?

Today, thank God that He is so fully worthy of your trust.

Day 2

Read Psalm 31:19–24. What does the psalmist say about courage in verse 24?

What reasons for courage does he cite in the earlier verses?

The psalmist speaks in verse 19 about fearing God. How is fearing God consistent with courage?

Have you ever felt like you were in a city under siege (see verse 21)? Describe that experience.

Tell God how grateful you are that you're not under siege. Or, if you do feel under siege, take this time to pour out your needs to Him.

Day 3

Read Philippians 1:27–30. How does Paul describe courageous living in this passage?

What are some examples of what is involved in living a life worthy of the gospel?

Why does God ask His people to suffer for Christ?

Has God asked you to suffer for His sake? If so, how is He helping you conduct yourself as you endure that painful situation?

Speak with God honestly regarding how you feel about suffering for Him.

Day 4

Read Isaiah 41:8–13. What reasons for courage does this passage offer?

Has God "chosen" you? How do you know?

If you know God has chosen you—and you have accepted His offer of salvation—how should this affect what you do when trouble comes?

Do you believe God when He says He will hold your hand and help you? Why or why not?

Thank God for the promises He gives to you in His Word, and offer yourself today for His service.

Day 5

Read Mark 15:42–46. Why did it take courage for Joseph of Arimathea to go to Pilate and ask for Jesus' body in order to bury it?

How was Joseph's situation similar to Esther's?

Why do you suppose Jesus' disciples weren't brave enough to go to Pilate and ask for the body?

What might have happened if no one had the courage to go to Pilate and ask for Jesus' body?

Ask God if there is something you need to be brave enough to do. Ask Him to guard you as you do it—and then thank Him that He promises to watch over you.

COURAGE TO PERSEVERE

CONSIDER IT

Courage isn't just for a moment; it is often something we must sustain for days, weeks, months, even years. And yet those periods of perseverance are really just a sustained series of steps—one after another. Ironically, the key to running the race of life with endurance is to concentrate on taking the next step, then the next, and then the next after that. In this session, we'll learn from the experience of a man who understood how to persevere in the face of opposition so he could accomplish the task set before him.

1. *How would you define perseverance?*

_____

_____

_____

2. *What situation in your life requires perseverance right now?*

_____

_____

_____

EXPERIENCE IT

"Come to Me, and rest in My loving Presence. You know that this day will bring difficulties, and you are trying to think your way through those trials. As you anticipate what is ahead of you, you forget that *I am with you*—now and always. Rehearsing your troubles results in experiencing them many times, whereas you are meant to go through them only when they actually occur. Do not multiply your suffering in this way! Instead, come to Me, and relax in My Peace. I will strengthen you and prepare you for this day, transforming your fear into confident trust."

—FROM *JESUS CALLING*, JANUARY 16

3. *What could be wrong with rehearsing your troubles? How is this different from appropriate planning?*

---

4. *How can resting and relaxing in God's Presence be good preparation for courageously getting things done?*

"*Trust Me, and don't be afraid.* Many things feel out of control. Your routines are not running smoothly. You tend to feel more secure when your life is predictable. Let Me lead you to *the rock that is higher than you* and your circumstances. *Take refuge in the shelter of My wings,* where you are absolutely secure.

"When you are shaken out of your comfortable routines, grip My hand tightly and look for growth opportunities. Instead of bemoaning the loss of your comfort, accept the challenge of something new. *I lead you on from glory to glory*, making you fit for My kingdom. Say *yes* to the ways I work in your life. Trust Me, and don't be afraid."

—FROM *JESUS CALLING*, APRIL 15

5. *Do you tend to feel more secure with predictable days? If so, how do you typically respond when your routines are upset? How do you want to respond?*

6. *What does it mean in practice to grip God's hand tightly?*

STUDY IT

Read aloud the following passage from Nehemiah 4:1–23. Note that this story takes place roughly thirty-five years after the story of Esther. The Persian Empire still ruled over Judah, but the Jews were now allowed to return from exile to resettle their land. Nehemiah was cupbearer to the Persian king—a highly trusted official who guaranteed the king's food and drink were free of poison.

When Nehemiah learned about the poor state of affairs in Jerusalem, he asked the king to allow him go back to Judah and lead the effort to rebuild the city wall. Cities needed walls in those days to be safe from attack. In the passage below, Nehemiah describes the opposition he and his wall-builders faced from enemies. Sanballat was governor of Samaria, the region just north of Judah. Samaria had controlled Judah for decades, but Nehemiah had now come as a special emissary from the Persian king and had been given authority to govern Judah.

[1] When Sanballat heard that we were rebuilding the wall, he became angry and was greatly incensed. He ridiculed the Jews, [2] and in the presence of his associates and the army of Samaria, he said, "What are those feeble Jews doing? Will they restore their wall? Will they offer sacrifices? Will they finish in a day? Can they bring the stones back to life from those heaps of rubble—burned as they are?"

[3] Tobiah the Ammonite, who was at his side, said, "What they are building—even a fox climbing up on it would break down their wall of stones!"

[4] Hear us, our God, for we are despised. Turn their insults back on their own heads. Give them over as plunder in a land of captivity. [5] Do not cover up their guilt or blot out their sins from your sight, for they have thrown insults in the face of the builders.

[6] So we rebuilt the wall till all of it reached half its height, for the people worked with all their heart.

[7] But when Sanballat, Tobiah, the Arabs, the Ammonites and the people of Ashdod heard that the repairs to Jerusalem's walls had gone ahead and that the gaps were being closed, they were very angry. [8] They all plotted together to come and fight against Jerusalem and stir up trouble against it. [9] But we prayed to our God and posted a guard day and night to meet this threat.

[10] Meanwhile, the people in Judah said, "The strength of the laborers is giving out, and there is so much rubble that we cannot rebuild the wall."

[11] Also our enemies said, "Before they know it or see us, we will be right there among them and will kill them and put an end to the work."

[12] Then the Jews who lived near them came and told us ten times over, "Wherever you turn, they will attack us."

[13] Therefore I stationed some of the people behind the lowest points of the wall at the exposed places, posting them by families, with their swords, spears and bows. [14] After I looked things over, I stood up and said to the nobles, the officials and the rest of the people, "Don't be afraid of them. Remember the Lord, who is great and awesome, and fight for your families, your sons and your daughters, your wives and your homes."

[15] When our enemies heard that we were aware of their plot and that God had frustrated it, we all returned to the wall, each to our own work.

[16] From that day on, half of my men did the work, while the other half were equipped with spears, shields, bows and armor. The officers posted themselves behind all the people of Judah [17] who were building the wall. Those who carried materials did their work with one hand and held a weapon in the other, [18] and each of the builders wore his sword at his side as he worked. But the man who sounded the trumpet stayed with me.

[19] Then I said to the nobles, the officials and the rest of the people, "The work is extensive and spread out, and we are widely separated from each other along the wall. [20] Wherever you hear the sound of the trumpet, join us there. Our God will fight for us!"

[21] So we continued the work with half the men holding spears, from the first light of dawn till the stars came out. [22] At that time I also said to the people, "Have every man and his helper stay inside Jerusalem at night, so they can serve us as guards by night and as workers by day." [23] Neither I nor my brothers nor my men nor the guards with me took off our clothes; each had his weapon, even when he went for water.

7. *What steps were involved in building a wall high enough to protect a city? Describe the process as you imagine it.*

8. *These builders had to deal with enemies while they worked. What did they do to deal with the threat?*

_____

_____

_____

9. *What do you think it would have been like to build a wall under those conditions? How would it have affected the speed of the work?*

_____

_____

_____

10. *In what ways did this situation require courage? Where did Nehemiah's courage come from? Where did the builders' courage come from?*

_____

_____

_____

_____

11. *Take two minutes of silence to reread Nehemiah 4:4–9, looking for a sentence, phrase, or even one word that stands out as something Jesus may want you to focus on in your life. If you're meeting with a group, the leader will keep track of time. At the end of two minutes, you may share your word or phrase with the group if you wish.*

12. *Read verses 4–9 aloud again. Take another two minutes of silence, prayerfully considering what response God might want you to make to what you have read in His Word. If you're meeting with a group, the leader will again keep track of time. At the end of two minutes, you may share what came to you in the silence if you wish.*

13. *If you're meeting with a group, how can the members pray for you? If you're using this study on your own, what would you like to say to God right now?*

LIVE IT

The theme of this week's daily Scripture readings is having courage to persevere when situations in your life become frustrating or difficult. Read each passage slowly, pausing to think about what is being said. Rather than approaching this as an assignment to complete, think of it as an opportunity to meet with the One who loves you most. Use any of the questions that are helpful.

Day 1

Read 2 Chronicles 32:1–8. What reasons for discouragement did the people of Judah have?

_____

_____

_____

_____

How did King Hezekiah encourage them?

_____

_____

_____

_____

_____

How could Hezekiah claim there were more forces on the side of Judah than on the side of Assyria, when King Sennacherib had the obviously bigger army?

_____

_____

_____

How is this like your situation today?

_____

_____

_____

Praise God for His faithfulness in fighting for His children.

Day 2

Read 2 Chronicles 32:9–19. What reasons did King Sennacherib give to the people of Judah as to why they should give up their courage?

_____

_____

_____

What was his argument? What did he say that was true? What did he say that was untrue?

_____

_____

_____

_____

Do you ever have a voice in your heart that says things like Sennacherib said? If so, how do you deal with that voice?

_____

_____

_____

What tactics did the Assyrians use in verses 18–19 to try to strike terror in the Jewish people's hearts? How does the enemy use these same tactics against you today?

_____

_____

_____

Thank the Lord for not being like the gods of the nations. Praise Him for giving you the strength to endure the taunts of the enemy and for helping you stand firm.

Day 3

Read 2 Chronicles 32:20–22. How did Hezekiah and Isaiah respond to the threat?

How did God defeat the Assyrian forces? What ultimately happened to Sennacherib?

What do you think it would have been like to be in the besieged city of Jerusalem and see this happen?

How important was Hezekiah's and the people's courage in the outcome of this conflict? For what in your life do you need to cry to heaven for help?

Give honor to God for His power and willingness to intervene on behalf of His sons and daughters who pray courageously.

Day 4

Read Deuteronomy 20:1–4. What reasons did Moses give the people for having courage in the midst of battle?

Why does Moses remind the people that God brought them up out of Egypt?

Why do you suppose the Bible has so many passages that give the same reason for courage?

_____

_____

_____

How does this message apply in your situation? What are the horses and chariots that are arrayed against you?

_____

_____

_____

Today, offer to God a prayer of confidence that He will fight for His children.

Day 5

Read Deuteronomy 20:5–8. In this next part of the story, Moses tells the military officers what to say to men of fighting age who are preparing for a battle. What is surprising about the speech the officers are supposed to give? Why would God want a smaller army?

_____

_____

_____

Why does God want people who lack courage to go home and not join the battle?

_____

_____

_____

In what ways does other people's courage or cowardice affect you?

_____

_____

_____

How can you be a good influence on the people around you when it comes to having courage to confront what you are facing?

_____

_____

_____

Be honest with God as to whether you tend to want to fight alongside Him or avoid the fight altogether. Ask Him to give you the courage to confront the battles you need to face.

COURAGE TO PROCLAIM THE GOSPEL

CONSIDER IT

We live in a society that is not always receptive to the claims of the gospel. Though it's legal and safe to practice our faith in private in North America, standing up for the gospel in public settings can lead to rejection and even trouble with the law. Sometimes family members or coworkers are hostile to the Christians in their midst.

In many countries around the world, Christians face a far more dangerous scenario: violence for private exercise of their faith, let alone for public proclamation. These believers need great courage just to call themselves followers of Christ. For us, the consequences of claiming Jesus as Lord are generally far less, yet we can be just as fearful of speaking up for Him. The fear of rejection and mockery is enough to silence us. In this session, we'll experience the boldness of the first followers of Jesus and see if some of their courage can rub off on us.

1. *Think of a time when you talked with a nonbeliever about Jesus. How courageous were you in expressing what you believe? What fears did you have to overcome?*

2. *What was the result of your conversation? If you could go back and do it over again, what would you change in your approach?*

EXPERIENCE IT

"Give yourself fully to the adventure of today. Walk boldly along the path of Life, relying on your ever-present Companion. You have every reason to be confident, because My Presence accompanies you all the days of your life—and onward into eternity.

"Do not give in to fear or worry, those robbers of abundant living. Trust Me enough to face problems as they come, rather than trying to anticipate them. *Fix your eyes on Me, the Author and Perfecter of your faith*, and many difficulties on the road ahead will vanish before you reach them. Whenever you start to feel afraid, remember that *I am holding you by your right hand*. Nothing can separate you from My Presence!"

—FROM *JESUS CALLING*, FEBRUARY 14

3. *What would it look like for you to give yourself fully to the adventure of today? What would you do? What attitude would you have?*

4. *What reasons for confidence do you have when you walk with Christ?*

"Do not let any set of circumstances intimidate you. The more challenging your day, the more of My Power I place at your disposal. You seem to think that I empower you equally each day, but this is not so. Your tendency upon awakening is to assess the difficulties ahead of you, measuring them against your average strength. This is an exercise in unreality.

"I know what each of your days will contain, and I empower you accordingly. The degree to which I strengthen you on a given day is based mainly on two variables: the difficulty of your circumstances, and your willingness to depend on Me for help. Try to view challenging days as opportunities to receive more of My Power than usual. Look to Me for all that you need, and watch to see what I will do. *As your day, so shall your strength be.*"

—From *Jesus Calling*, November 11

5. *How do you respond to the idea that the more challenging your day, the more God places His Power at your disposal? In what ways have you experienced this as a believer?*

6. *What motivates you to depend on Jesus for help? What could keep a person from depending on Jesus for assistance?*

STUDY IT

Read aloud the following passage from Acts 4:1–31. Note that as the events in this passage unfold, the disciples Peter and John have seen the resurrected Jesus and have received the empowering of the Holy Spirit so that they may testify to what they have seen. The Holy Spirit has also empowered them to miraculously heal people the way Jesus did, and they have healed a lame beggar at the temple in Jerusalem. This healing has attracted a crowd, and Peter has been speaking to the crowd about Jesus. The story picks up as the priests who control the temple interrupt Peter's speech. The leading men of the city (the Sanhedrin, made up of synagogue rulers, elders, teachers of the law, and members of the high priest's family) are the same men who had persuaded the Roman governor to execute Jesus just a couple of months earlier.

[1] The priests and the captain of the temple guard and the Sadducees came up to Peter and John while they were speaking to the people. [2] They were greatly disturbed because the apostles were teaching the people, proclaiming in Jesus the resurrection of the dead. [3] They seized Peter and John and, because it was evening, they put them in jail until the next day. [4] But many who heard the message believed; so the number of men who believed grew to about five thousand.

[5] The next day the rulers, the elders and the teachers of the law met in Jerusalem. [6] Annas the high priest was there, and so were Caiaphas, John, Alexander and others of the high priest's family. [7] They had Peter and John brought before them and began to question them: "By what power or what name did you do this?"

[8] Then Peter, filled with the Holy Spirit, said to them: "Rulers and elders of the people! [9] If we are being called to account today for an act of kindness shown to a man who was lame and are being asked how he was healed, [10] then know this, you and all the people of Israel: It is by the name of Jesus Christ of Nazareth, whom you crucified but whom God raised from the dead, that this man stands before you healed. [11] Jesus is

'the stone you builders rejected,

which has become the cornerstone.'

[12] Salvation is found in no one else, for there is no other name under heaven given to mankind by which we must be saved."

[13] When they saw the courage of Peter and John and realized that they were unschooled, ordinary men, they were astonished and they took note that these men had been with Jesus. [14] But since they could see the man who had been healed standing there with them, there was nothing they could say. [15] So they ordered them to withdraw from the Sanhedrin and then conferred together. [16] "What are we going to do with these men?" they asked. "Everyone living in Jerusalem knows they have performed a notable sign, and we cannot deny it. [17] But to stop this thing from spreading any further among the people, we must warn them to speak no longer to anyone in this name."

[18] Then they called them in again and commanded them not to speak or teach at all in the name of Jesus. [19] But Peter and John replied, "Which is right in God's eyes: to listen to you, or to him? You be the judges! [20] As for us, we cannot help speaking about what we have seen and heard."

[21] After further threats they let them go. They could not decide how to punish them, because all the people were praising God for what had happened. [22] For the man who was miraculously healed was over forty years old.

[23] On their release, Peter and John went back to their own people and reported all that the chief priests and the elders had said to them. [24] When they heard this, they raised their voices together in prayer to God. "Sovereign Lord," they said, "you made the heavens and the earth and the sea, and everything in them. [25] You spoke by the Holy Spirit through the mouth of your servant, our father David:

"'Why do the nations rage
    and the peoples plot in vain?

^{26} The kings of the earth rise up
    and the rulers band together
against the Lord
    and against his anointed one.'

^{27} Indeed Herod and Pontius Pilate met together with the Gentiles and the people of Israel in this city to conspire against your holy servant Jesus, whom you anointed. ^{28} They did what your power and will had decided beforehand should happen. ^{29} Now, Lord, consider their threats and enable your servants to speak your word with great boldness. ^{30} Stretch out your hand to heal and perform signs and wonders through the name of your holy servant Jesus."

^{31} After they prayed, the place where they were meeting was shaken. And they were all filled with the Holy Spirit and spoke the word of God boldly.

7. *What did Peter and John do that took courage? Why did this take courage?*

_____

_____

_____

8. *Peter and John said, "We cannot help speaking about what we have seen and heard." Why couldn't they help it?*

_____

_____

_____

9. *Peter and John went back to the other believers, and then the whole group prayed together. For what did they pray? How would you describe the attitude they expressed when they prayed?*

10. *Why are Christians today often reluctant to speak about their experience of Jesus, even though it is much safer for them than it was for Peter and John? What are the risks of asking God to enable you to speak His word with boldness? What are the benefits?*

11. *Take two minutes of silence to reread Acts 4:18–20, looking for a sentence, phrase, or even one word that stands out as something Jesus may want you to focus on in your life. If you're meeting with a group, the leader will keep track of time. At the end of two minutes, you may share your word or phrase with the group if you wish.*

12. *Read verses 18–20 aloud again. Take another two minutes of silence, prayerfully considering what response God might want you to make to what you have read in His Word. If you're meeting with a group, the leader will again keep track of time. At the end of two minutes, you may share what came to you in the silence if you wish.*

13. *If you're meeting with a group, how can the members pray for you? If you're using this study on your own, what would you like to say to God right now?*

LIVE IT

The theme of this week's daily Scripture readings is having courage to share the message of Christ. Each day, you will look at some events that unfolded in the early church after Peter and John stood up to the Sanhedrin. Read each passage slowly, pausing to think about what is being said. Rather than approaching this as an assignment to complete, think of it as an opportunity to meet with the One who loves you most. Use any of the questions that are helpful.

Day 1

Read Acts 5:12–21. What reasons did the believers have to fear?

What reasons did they have to be courageous?

Why do you think courage won out for them? How did they display that courage?

What reasons do you have to be afraid? What reasons do you have to be courageous?

Make the decision today to live with courage instead of fear. Offer yourself to God to be used in whatever way He desires for His kingdom.

Day 2

Read Acts 5:21–40. How did God protect the apostles?

God allowed them to be flogged (verse 40), which meant they were stripped to the waist and whipped thirty-nine times. What do you expect the flogging did to their courage? Why?

How would being flogged have affected your willingness to proclaim the gospel? Why?

What does this passage make you want to ask from God?

_____

_____

_____

_____

Pray for courage today to confront whatever tries to oppose your sharing of the message of Christ. Ask God to help you focus on the big picture of bringing people into His kingdom.

Day 3

Read Acts 5:41–42. What was the apostles' surprising response to the flogging? Why do you think they responded in this way?

_____

_____

_____

Could you rejoice if you were counted worthy to suffer disgrace for Jesus' sake? What would make this especially difficult for you to do?

_____

_____

_____

COURAGE TO PROCLAIM THE GOSPEL

What could help you find joy in such a circumstance?

_____

_____

_____

In what ways have you suffered disgrace (or worse) for Jesus' sake?

_____

_____

_____

Today, ask God to help you be willing to suffer disgrace for Jesus' sake. Seek His help to find joy in every situation, knowing that He is always with His followers and guiding them forward.

Day 4

Read Acts 6:8–15. Stephen had been appointed by the twelve disciples to minister to the widows in the daily distribution of food (see Acts 6:1). How is Stephen described in this passage?

_____

_____

_____

_____

In what ways was Stephen in danger? Why was he in danger?

_____

_____

_____

Given what has happened up to this point in Acts, would you expect Stephen to be protected from harm? Why or why not?

_____

_____

_____

How was Stephen in a situation much like the three young men in Daniel 3? How does his example affect your courage?

_____

_____

_____

Ask the Lord to give you courage like Stephen possessed to proclaim His truth.

Day 5

Read Acts 7:1–2 and 51–60 (or the whole chapter, if you prefer). What happened to Stephen because of his courageous preaching?

Why do you think God didn't protect Stephen the way he had earlier protected Peter and John?

Would you expect Stephen's fate to make the believers more afraid of speaking up about Jesus? Why or why not?

How can Stephen's story inspire you with courage?

Honestly tell God how you feel about being in His service. Continue to pray for the courage and willingness to share the good news of Christ with a lost and hurting world.

COURAGE TO WITHSTAND THE EVIL ONE

CONSIDER IT

The Bible describes Satan as "a roaring lion" who prowls around "looking for someone to devour" (1 Peter 5:8). Like any predator, he seeks to exploit weaknesses, cultivate fear, and isolate his victims so he can take them captive and destroy them. The evil one wants to bring down God's children and separate them from the intimacy with Jesus that is their birthright. The enemy has great power . . . but we must remember that Jesus has *greater* power. And as we learn to stand firm in Christ's strength, we are able to overcome every deception and attack our adversary can inflict on us. In this final session, we'll explore how we can develop the courage to stand even against the devil himself.

1. *What comes to mind when you picture Satan as a roaring lion who is constantly looking for someone to devour? What fears does that create in you?*

2. *In the Bible the Lord is also depicted as a lion—the "Lion of Judah" who protects His people. What difference does that make for you when it comes to facing the enemy?*

EXPERIENCE IT

"*Trust Me, and don't be afraid.* I want you to view trials as exercises designed to develop your trust-muscles. You live in the midst of fierce spiritual battles, and fear is one of Satan's favorite weapons. When you start to feel afraid, affirm your trust in Me. Speak out loud, if circumstances permit. *Resist the devil in My Name, and he will slink away from you.* Refresh yourself in My holy Presence. Speak or sing praises to Me, and My Face will shine radiantly upon you.

"Remember that there is no condemnation for those who belong to Me. You have been judged not guilty for all eternity. Trust Me, and don't be afraid; for I am your Strength, Song, and Salvation."

—FROM *JESUS CALLING*, AUGUST 22

3. *How does Satan use fear as a weapon against you?*

_____

_____

_____

4. *How can you actively resist Satan when he attacks you with fear?*

_____

_____

_____

"Do not be surprised by the fiery attacks on your mind. When you struggle to find Me and to live in My Peace, don't let discouragement set in. You are engaged in massive warfare, spiritually speaking. The evil

one abhors your closeness to Me, and his demonic underlings are determined to destroy our intimacy. When you find yourself in the thick of
battle, call upon My Name: 'Jesus, help me!' At that instant, the battle
becomes Mine; your role is simply to trust Me as I fight for you.

"My Name, properly used, has unlimited Power to bless and protect. At the end of time, *every knee will bow (in heaven, on earth, and
under the earth) when My Name is proclaimed*. People who have used
'Jesus' as a shoddy swear word will fall down in terror on that awesome
day. But all those who have drawn near Me through trustingly uttering
My Name will be filled with *inexpressible and glorious Joy*. This is your
great hope, as you await My return."

—FROM *JESUS CALLING*, DECEMBER 3

5. *According to what you know of Scripture, how does the evil one attack your
mind?*

6. *What are some ways to engage in warfare against Satan?*

STUDY IT

Read aloud the following passage from Ephesians 6:10–20. In these verses, the apostle Paul draws on the example of a Roman soldier to show how we should prepare ourselves to battle against the attacks of the enemy.

[10] Finally, be strong in the Lord and in his mighty power. [11] Put on the full armor of God, so that you can take your stand against the devil's schemes. [12] For our struggle is not against flesh and blood, but against the rulers, against the authorities, against the powers of this dark world and against the spiritual forces of evil in the heavenly realms. [13] Therefore put on the full armor of God, so that when the day of evil comes, you may be able to stand your ground, and after you have done everything, to stand. [14] Stand firm then, with the belt of truth buckled around your waist, with the breastplate of righteousness in place, [15] and with your feet fitted with the readiness that comes from the gospel of peace. [16] In addition to all this, take up the shield of faith, with which you can extinguish all the flaming arrows of the evil one. [17] Take the helmet of salvation and the sword of the Spirit, which is the word of God.

[18] And pray in the Spirit on all occasions with all kinds of prayers and requests. With this in mind, be alert and always keep on praying for all the Lord's people. [19] Pray also for me, that whenever I speak, words may be given me so that I will fearlessly make known the mystery of the gospel, [20] for which I am an ambassador in chains. Pray that I may declare it fearlessly, as I should.

7. How do the following pieces of armor equip you to stand against the enemy's schemes?

Belt of Truth:

Breastplate of Righteousness:

Shoes of the Gospel of Peace:

Shield of Faith:

Helmet of Salvation:

Sword of the Spirit:

8. *Why do you think Paul focuses in this passage on the believer's ability to stand firm against the enemy rather than going on the offensive and trying to attack the enemy?*

9. *What do you learn about the power of prayer in verses 18–20? How does this qualify as standing against the enemy?*

10. *What statements in this passage inspire your courage?*

11. *Take two minutes of silence to reread the passage, looking for a sentence, phrase, or even one word that stands out as something Jesus may want you to focus on in your life. If you're meeting with a group, the leader will keep track of time. At the end of two minutes, you may share your word or phrase with the group if you wish.*

12. *Read the passage aloud again. Take another two minutes of silence, prayerfully considering what response God might want you to make to what you have read in His Word. If you're meeting with a group, the leader will again keep track of time. At the end of two minutes, you may share what came to you in the silence if you wish.*

13. *If you're meeting with a group, how can the members pray for you? If you're using this study on your own, what would you like to say to God right now?*

LIVE IT

The theme of this week's daily Scripture readings is how you can put on the armor of God to boldly resist the attacks of the enemy. Read each passage slowly, pausing to think about what is being said. Rather than approaching this as an assignment to complete, think of it as an opportunity to meet with the One who loves you most. Use any of the questions that are helpful.

Day 1

Read Matthew 4:18–22. Why did it require courage on the part of Peter, Andrew, James, and John to leave their livelihoods behind and follow Jesus?

What have you given up in your life to follow Jesus?

What have you gained by following Christ?

Do you have any regrets about the things you've given up? Explain.

Take a few moments to thank God for inviting you onto the adventurous path of following Him.

Day 2

Read James 1:5–8. As a follower of Christ, do you ever doubt the path that He has set for you? How do you deal with doubt?

In what ways has self-doubt hindered your courage?

What about doubt that Jesus would protect you—has that ever hindered your courage? If so, how did you deal with it?

How can believers in Christ help each other deal with doubts?

Tell God today about your doubts—and be honest! Ask Him to give you wisdom and the courage to act on whatever He might reveal to you.

Day 3

Read Acts 9:10–19. Why did Ananias need courage to obey God? What risk was he taking?

What do you think would have happened if Ananias had refused to take this risk?

When have you witnessed someone acting courageously for Christ? How does it affect you to read about Christians who take such big risks?

What risk—even a small one—might God be asking of you today?

Tell God your ears are open to His guidance to do His work in the world.

Day 4

Read Acts 9:19–30. What risks did Saul take? How can you tell he was courageous?

Do you think Paul took excessive risk, given that his followers had to smuggle him out of where he was living? Why or why not?

In what ways are you reluctant to speak up about your faith for fear of rejection?

How does Paul's story ignite your courage?

_____

_____

_____

_____

Ask God for the wisdom today to know the time, place, and method for sharing your faith in Christ with others.

Day 5

Read Acts 12:1–11. What happened to James in this passage? What happened to Peter?

_____

_____

_____

Does God's ability and willingness to rescue Peter strengthen your courage? Why or why not?

_____

_____

_____

Does God's willingness to let James suffer get in the way of your courage? Why or why not?

_____

_____

_____

What should we learn from the fates of James and Peter in this story?

_____

_____

_____

Affirm to God that you trust Him to keep your soul safe no matter what happens to your physical body.

LEADER'S NOTES

Thank you for your willingness to lead a group through this *Jesus Calling* study. The rewards of leading are different from the rewards of participating, and we hope you find your own walk with Jesus deepened by this experience. In many ways, your group meetings will be structured like other Bible studies in which you've participated. You'll want to open in prayer, for example, and ask people to silence their phones. These leader's notes will focus on elements of the study that may be new to you.

CONSIDER IT

This first portion of the study functions as an icebreaker. It gets the group members thinking about the topic at hand by asking them to share from their own experience. Some people may be tempted to tell a long story in response to one of these questions, but the goal is to keep the answers brief. Ideally, you want everyone in the group to have a chance to answer the *Consider It* questions, so you may want to explain up front that everyone needs to limit his or her answer to one minute.

With the rest of the study, it is generally not a good idea to go around the circle and have everyone answer every question—a free-flowing discussion is more desirable. But with the *Consider It* questions, you can go around the circle. Encourage shy people to share, but don't force them. Tell the group they should feel free to pass if they prefer not to answer a question.

EXPERIENCE IT

This is the group's chance to talk about excerpts from the *Jesus Calling* devotional. You will need to monitor this discussion closely so that you have enough time for the actual study of God's Word that follows. If the group has a long and rich discussion on one of the devotional excerpts, you may choose to skip the other one and move on to the Bible study. Don't feel obliged to cover every *Experience It* question if the conversation is fruitful. On the other hand, do move on if the group gets off on a tangent.

STUDY IT

Try to do the *Study It* exercise in session 1 on your own before the group meets the first time so you can coach people on what to expect. Note that this section may be a little different from Bible studies your group has done in the past. The group will talk about the Bible passage as usual, but then there will be several minutes of silence so individuals can pray about what God might want to say to them personally through the reading. It will be up to you to keep track of the time and call people back together when the time is up. (There are some good timer apps that play a gentle chime or other pleasant sound instead of a disruptive noise.) If the group members aren't used to being silent in a "crowd," brief them on what to expect.

Don't be afraid to let people sit in silence. Two minutes of quiet may seem like a long time at first, but it will help to train group members to sit in silence with God when they are alone. They can remain where they are in the circle, or if you have space, you can let them go off by themselves to other rooms at your instruction. If your group meets in a home, ask the host before the meeting which rooms are available for use. Some people will be more comfortable in the quiet if they have a bit of space from others.

When the group reconvenes after the time of silence, invite them to share what they experienced. There are several questions provided in this study guide that you can ask. Note that it's not necessary to cover every question if the group has a good discussion going. It's also not necessary to go around the circle and make everyone share.

Don't be concerned if the group members are reserved and slow to share after the exercise. People are often quiet when they are pulling together their ideas, and the exercise will have been a new experience for many of them. Just ask a question and let it hang in the air until someone speaks up. You can then say, "Thank you. What about others? What came to you when you sat with the passage?"

Some people may say they found it hard to quiet their minds enough to focus on the passage for those few minutes. Tell them this is okay. They're practicing a skill, and sometimes skills take time to learn. If they learn to sit quietly with God's Word in a group, they will become much more comfortable sitting with the Word on their own. Remind them that spending time in the Bible each day is one of the most valuable things they can do as believers in Christ.

PREPARATION

It's not necessary for group members to prepare anything for the study ahead of time. However, at the end of each study are five days' worth of suggestions for spending time in God's Word during the next week. These daily times are optional but valuable, so encourage the group to do them. Also, invite them to bring their questions and insights to the group at your next meeting, especially if they had a breakthrough moment or if they didn't understand something.

As the leader, there are a few things you should do to prepare for each meeting:

- *Read through the session.* This will help you become familiar with the content and know how to structure the discussion times.

- *Spend five to ten minutes doing the* Study It *questions on your own.* When the group meets, you'll be watching the clock, so you'll probably have a more fulfilling time with the passage if you do the exercise ahead of time. You can then spend time in the passage again with the group. This way, you'll be sure to have the key verses for that session deeply in your mind.

- *Pray for your group.* Pray especially that God will guide them into a deeper understanding of how they can be thankful to Him in every area of life.

- *Bring extra supplies to your meeting.* Group members should bring their own pens for writing notes on the Bible reflection, but it is a good idea to have extras available for those who forget. You may also want to bring paper and Bibles for those who may have neglected to bring their study guides to the meeting.

Below you will find suggested answers for some of the study questions. Note that in many cases there is no one right answer, especially when group members are sharing their personal experiences.

Session 1: Courage to Obey the Lord's Instructions

1. *Some examples include a firefighter rushing into a burning building, a warrior in armor, or a person who stands up for his or her beliefs. The goal here is to get the group members thinking about what courage means to them.*

They may not necessarily see the need for courage in their own lives if they are thinking of it only as something that is essential for people in certain professions or roles.

2. *Answers will vary. Ideally, the discussion will lead the group members to conclude that everyone needs courage to take action, whether it's standing up for what is right, or going against what is popular, or reaching out to those who might reject them.*

3. *Some examples of things that will foster a sense of peace in our hearts include a steady diet of Scripture and a habit of sitting down in a quiet place every day to just be still with God. Our minds may wander at first, but if we persevere, the stillness will become more engrained, enabling us to be at peace throughout the day, and especially when we need to overcome anxiety.*

4. *Those in the media make their money by getting our attention—and they get our attention by reporting news that arouses negative emotions (especially fear and anger). Over time, this constant, fear-based bombardment eats away at our courage and makes us feel helpless in a seemingly out-of-control world. This, in turn, distracts us from the situations where we can make a real difference for the good! However, when we tune into the Word of God, we are reminded that nothing on this earth is ever out of His hands. God has instructed His people to "fear not" for a reason—because He is constantly with them!*

5. *Answers will vary. Share a story from your own life of a time when you went out on a limb—and survived to tell the tale! Even if what happened wasn't ideal, it didn't kill you. You might also emphasize that those who love God and follow after Him never go alone—He goes before them and behind them and beside them. These reminders will encourage the group members to believe that Jesus can be trusted.*

6. *Some of us are certainly more open to risk-taking than others, but the truth is that being close to Jesus will inevitably require each of us to go beyond our* *comfort zone. We may desire a risk-free life, but Jesus commands us as His disciples to follow wherever He leads. Thankfully, this is actually the safest place of all, for we know that He walks with us and orders our every step.*

7. *The Israelites needed courage to cross the Jordan River, fight the inhabitants of the Promised Land, and take possession of the territory God had reserved for them. Joshua needed the courage to lead them in that fight.*

8. *For the Israelites and their leader, their courage was based on God's promises to go with them and to never leave or forsake them. The Lord had promised He would fight for them and destroy the nations they were about to confront. God has promised the same to us—that He will never leave or forsake us. If He has given us a task to complete, He will faithfully supply the strength to complete it.*

9. *Answers will vary. God's promises of His Presence and His help can strengthen us with the assurance that, as believers, we are never on our own when it comes to a challenging situation. Someone much bigger and stronger is doing the heavy lifting! His ever-present help also sustains us when we start to grow weary or discouraged.*

10. *Answers will vary. It's fine for this process to be unfamiliar to the group at first. Be sure to keep track of time.*

11. *Answers will vary.*

12. *Answers will vary. Note that some people may find the silence intimidating initially. Their anxiety might tempt them to fill the air with noise, but it will be helpful for these group members to just take a quiet moment before God. Let them express their discomfort once you're all gathered together again, but make sure it is balanced by those who found the silence strengthening. Helping people become comfortable with this "holy quiet" will serve their private daily times with God in wonderful ways.*

13. *Take as much time as you can to pray for each other. You might have someone write down the prayer requests so you can keep track of answers to prayer.*

Session 2: Courage to Confront a Stronger Force

1. *Answers will vary. This could be something as simple as someone's first day of school.*

2. *Allow the group members some time to share about their response to the situation.*

3. *Fear causes us to focus on the negative things in our situation—the things we can't change—rather than on the things that God is actively doing in our midst. When we allow fear to take over, it blocks us from seeing how God is pouring His strength into us on a daily basis.*

4. *Fighting fear means our brains are still focused on fear; thus, we are just reinforcing those consuming, paralyzing thoughts. Instead, we need to turn our minds where they belong: toward God and His unfailing character. He can be trusted to be our help in times of trouble.*

5. *When faced with difficulties, what you should do is: (1) remember that God is with you, (2) speak with Him, and (3) listen as He talks you through the situation. What you shouldn't do is panic, fear your limitations, or measure the day's demands against your own strength. The Lord won't necessarily give you a complete road map through the difficulty all at once. However, what He will do is be with you and guide you step-by-step through the situation.*

6. *Some of us tend to panic or get anxious. Some of us try to power through the difficulty, making decisions without consulting God. Neither of these responses is a good one, because both leave us ill-equipped for difficulties that are truly too much for us.*

7. *The text doesn't explicitly state what gave Goliath courage, but it appears he trusted in his height, strength, armor, and weapons (which are detailed in verses 5–7), and superior abilities as a warrior. Goliath may also have relied on his gods (mentioned briefly in verse 43).*

8. *David's courage to fight came from the Lord. He gave God credit for saving him from wild animals, and he said the Lord was the one who would defeat Goliath. David was courageous because he acted in the name of the Lord, not because he was confident in his own abilities or skills. He declined the offer of Saul's armor because he knew it would hinder him.*

9. *God works through ordinary people so that onlookers will see that He—not the human—is the one who deserves the credit and provides the power for the achievement.*

10. *The story is compelling because young David was bold in the face of an obviously stronger and better-equipped foe. The way David wins—with a slingshot—also appeals to our delight when the underdog wins. We reason that if the Lord enabled David to pull off this victory, He could enable us to do the same when we're facing "giants" in our lives.*

11. *Answers will vary.*

12. *Answers will vary.*

13. *Responses will vary.*

Session 3: Courage to Say No to False Gods

1. *Answers might include a boss, a parent, a spouse, a friend, or even a child. For example, it's natural for children to believe the world revolves around them and their needs. It's a parent's job to help their children outgrow this narcissism, learn that other people's needs matter, and recognize God as God.*

For adults, there is no excuse for self-absorption. Tantrums and manipulation are two ways people express a desire to be treated like God.

2. *Most likely there was some type of cost involved in putting God first, whether that was a loss of income, status, time, friendship, or some personal comfort.*

3. *It's normal to try to bury or deny feelings of incompleteness, so help your group members get in touch with the ways they do this. It might be as simple as keeping the television running when they are alone, excessive use of social media, or relying on another individual. This is one of the ways we fall into idolatry—we cling to the idolized person or activity in an effort to fill ourselves up.*

4. *Things that help us go to God with our neediness include a daily practice of time spent with Him in prayer, reading His Word, and the support of Christian friends. Things that get in the way include pride, fear, and busyness. Look for ways to overcome the obstacles that group members name.*

5. *We may depend on a job for our financial security, or on a spouse, friend, or family member for companionship. These are good things, but if they take God's place as our source of security, they are idols—unreliable idols. The first step in overcoming any unhealthy dependency is to notice how much we lean on that person or object. We can confess our dependencies to God and ask Him to help us turn to Him first and foremost.*

6. *Since we can't physically see Him or touch Him, depending on Him can feel a bit like falling backward, hoping we will be caught. In John 20:29, Jesus told His disciple Thomas, who had doubts that He was resurrected, "Because you have seen me [physically], you have believed; blessed are those who have not seen and yet have believed." It takes courage to put our full weight, so to speak, on Someone who is beyond our physical senses.*

7. *The three young men had to be brave enough to resist the king's command to bow down to an idol, knowing that the penalty for refusing was death.*

8. *God wanted the three men to live their faith in public, not just in private. Faith isn't only the personal sphere of our lives—it's hypocritical for us to be one thing in public and another in private. Shadrach, Meshach, and Abednego could conform to the expectations of the pagan culture to a certain degree, but they had to draw the line at giving any appearance of worshiping a false god.*

9. *The men affirmed that God was able to deliver them from death and also willing to do so. At the same time, they affirmed that He was under no obligation to do what they wanted. He would still be a good God, worthy of exclusive worship, even if He allowed them to die as martyrs. In this we see that Shadrach, Meshach, and Abednego weren't brave because they were promised that God would save them, but because they completely trusted in Him regardless of the outcome. Their words reveal the realism of their courage.*

10. *Courage isn't courage if the happy ending in this life is guaranteed. We know that God can do anything, but we also know that He's not obligated to do what we want. In the long run, Christians are promised eternal life, but in this life, we have to be brave without guarantees.*

11. *Answers will vary.*

12. *Answers will vary.*

13. *Responses will vary.*

Session 4: Courage to Withstand Others' Envy

1. *Give the group members some time to briefly share their stories of demonstrated courage from the past few weeks and what form that took in their lives.*

2. *The goal is to encourage group members to watch for opportunities to live with courage as they go through their days. It might be embarrassing for them to say, "I was brave when I did this small thing," but remind them that even small acts of courage are inspiring.*

3. *Adversity can make us bitter or better, and we choose which will take root in our lives. If we move toward God in times of adversity, admitting our need for Him, it propels us to grow in grace. We can become more patient, more hopeful, more humble.*

4. *Trust produces and feeds courage. If we don't trust God, we are naturally left with fear when we're out of our element. However, the more we trust God, the more able we are to consistently make courageous choices—even when they require risk.*

5. *When we look ahead to a problem down the road, we stop paying attention to what is right at our feet. We don't know whether we'll really have to scale the cliffs we see in the distance, or whether there is a route around them that God wants us to take. Following Jesus one step at a time helps us to not worry needlessly about the future, but rather to give our best to this day.*

6. *Everyone is facing something that requires some measure of courage. If the group members don't see any situation in their lives right now that requires courage, ask them what tasks they have on their plate right now. See if you can help them identify the places where they need to really be following Jesus one step at a time.*

7. *Both stories are about faithful Jewish men being willing to face death rather than compromising their worship of the one true God. In both cases also, jealous government officials (astrologers were government officials in Babylon) betrayed their Jewish colleagues. But there are some differences. First, King Nebuchadnezzar wanted people to worship his idol, while King Darius was tricked into making a law that ensnared Daniel. Second, in this* situation, Daniel was deliberately targeted because his fellow officials were envious of his position and wanted to bring him down.

8. Daniel did his work with such excellence that the king wanted to promote him. This meant that Daniel would gain power while his fellow officials would lose some power. So they acted out of a desire to protect their turf.

9. Some group members may never have been targets of bullying, but others likely will have been. As the members share, be sure to not pass judgment about the various ways they responded. Dealing with bullying is extremely hard if there is no authority figure to whom a person can appeal for help. Fighting back isn't always possible.

10. Daniel could have gone to the king for an exemption, but because he knew the law couldn't be repealed, he may have judged that choice to be useless. Or he could have stopped his private worship for thirty days, figuring, "It's only thirty days, after all." This would have been the "smart" thing to do if he didn't think daily prayer and a firm belief in God were essential. However, these were so important to Daniel that he wouldn't stop praying or trusting the Lord for even one day.

11. Answers will vary.

12. Answers will vary.

13. Responses will vary.

Session 5: Courage to Protest Against Wrong

1. Answers will vary. To a certain extent, boldness is a personality trait that some of us have in abundance and others have in smaller quantities. Yet God honors courage in the naturally quiet person who has to depend on Him for the faith to speak up—He doesn't just value the boldness of those for whom it comes more naturally.

2. *Hopefully, the story in this week's session will help group members be more aware of, and act on, opportunities they have to stand up for others—even when risk is involved.*

3. *"Walking by sight" means living according to what we can see and reason out—we make decisions based on how things look to us. "Walking by faith" means making decisions based solely on what God says about our situation. It means living courageously because we trust God to have our best interests at heart.*

4. *We don't need to live our lives too safely because the Holy Spirit empowers us as believers to live beyond our natural ability and strength. Some evidence of living "too safe" might be if we find we never need to depend on Him for the strength to make a difference in the world, or if we never feel the need to take a risk to further His work, or if we are just going through the "motions" of being a Christian, or if we lack passion in seeing others come to Christ.*

5. *While not everyone in the group will have faced such a situation, hopefully the stories of those who have will encourage everyone. Try to think ahead of time about a situation you faced where you needed to boldly depend on God—perhaps for even something as straightforward as leading this group!*

6. *The evidence for craving an easy life includes avoiding or complaining about difficulties instead of crying out to God, failing to confront them squarely, and evading opportunities to serve God because those opportunities seem scary.*

7. *Esther didn't have what we would regard as a "normal" marriage. She lived in a harem, and she could see the king only when he summoned her. So it was a huge risk for her to approach him. She then had to take another big risk in asking the king to circumvent the law he had passed that gave Haman permission to kill the Jews. She had no idea how her very unpredictable husband would respond in either case.*

8. *Esther and her family might have been killed as part of the mass slaughter of Jews that Haman had received permission to carry out.*

9. *The author of the book of Esther seems to have deliberately avoided mentioning God, worship, and prayer so the reader would have to look for Him. The three-day fast would have accompanied prayers for God to intervene and protect the Jews from destruction. Mordecai also implied that God was behind the king's choice of Esther as queen. God sometimes works unseen in the events of our lives.*

10. *At least some in the group will have had an experience of being in the right place at the right time to speak out for others and help them. Ask them to share these stories and even think of ways they might have overlooked God's hand in placing them where they could serve others.*

11. *Answers will vary.*

12. *Answers will vary.*

13. *Responses will vary.*

Session 6: Courage to Persevere

1. *The Merriam-Webster dictionary defines perseverance as "continued effort to do or achieve something despite difficulties, failure, or opposition." The key factors are difficulties and continued effort.*

2. *Answers will vary. Allow the group members to share some examples from their lives that require patience and perseverance at the present time.*

3. *"Rehearsing" troubles results in experiencing the negative over and over. As we'll see during this week's Bible study in Nehemiah, there is a way to take appropriate action to deal with troubles and then get on with the work,* without obsessing over the troubles. *Planning focuses us on actions we can take. Rehearsing takes no action; it keeps us stuck.*

4. *If, for example, we take time early in the day to rest in God's Presence, it sets us up for going through even a difficult day more peacefully. Whenever our courage is challenged, we can return to that inner place of rest. We will then have the presence of mind throughout the day to accomplish the tasks that are set before us.*

5. *Many people get agitated when their routines are upset. This is normal, but it can be overcome. It helps if we truly believe deep down that God is in control of the circumstances. We can cultivate that belief by regularly going to Him day by day and reminding ourselves that nothing we face in this day will catch Him by surprise.*

6. *Gripping God's hand tightly means to turn our minds resolutely toward Him and affirm the biblical truth that He is in control. We might even say, "Jesus, I trust You" consistently throughout the day as the Holy Spirit prompts us.*

7. *First, it was necessary for the Jews to clear away the rubble from the demolished wall. Some of the old stones could have been reused, but much of the rubble would have been too crushed to be of use, and new stone would have to be cut and hauled in from elsewhere. An enormous amount of stone was needed to build a wall at least twenty feet high that stretched for miles around a city. Good mortar was also necessary to fix the stones in place. This was a big job that required the volunteer labor of hundreds of people!*

8. *The builders relied on God and also took practical steps to protect themselves: "We prayed to our God and posted a guard day and night to meet this threat" (verse 9). Nehemiah stationed armed men and told them, "Don't be afraid of them. Remember the LORD, who is great and awesome, and fight for your families, your sons and your daughters, your wives and your homes" (verse 14). Nehemiah also had the builders carry weapons while they were working. His* *ultimate trust was in God, which he showed by his commitment to prayer and his encouragement that God would fight for them. Yet he wasn't naive about the need for practical measures as well. Above all, Nehemiah didn't cave in to fear.*

9. *Building a stone wall is backbreaking work under the best of conditions. The work would certainly have been much slower and more difficult if the builders were required to carry weapons and brace themselves for attack at all times.*

10. *Even without enemies threatening, it required courage on the Jews' part—given the size of the undertaking—to believe the wall could be rebuilt by laypeople. When hostile neighbors threatened to attack, it would have required even more courage to trust that God would prevent or defeat the opposition. Nehemiah says in verse 20, "Our God will fight for us." His courage came from his confidence in God. The builders seem to have been trusting God as well, and were probably spurred on by their leader's brave faith and example.*

11. *Answers will vary.*

12. *Answers will vary.*

13. *Responses will vary.*

Session 7: Courage to Proclaim the Gospel

1. *Most Christians have had at least one talk with a nonbeliever about Jesus, even if that conversation was mostly listening to the person's reasons for rejecting Christ. Some fears to overcome include the possibility of ridicule, judgment, rejection, or being the target of the other person's anger.*

2. *Answers will vary. Unfortunately, even one uncomfortable experience can be enough to discourage us if we are sensitive to rejection. God wants to help His people overcome that discouragement.*

3. *Some examples including doing a task that we have been putting off, engaging with a person we might normally pass by, or staying present with Jesus via brief prayers throughout the day.*

4. *The Bible says we can be confident when we walk with Christ because we have the assurance that He will be present with us every moment of every day—and that He will be present with us into eternity. God is holding our hand. He is already taking care of difficulties on the road ahead.*

5. *In Isaiah 40:31, God promises, "Those who hope in the LORD will renew their strength. They will soar on wings like eagles; they will run and not grow weary, they will walk and not be faint." The more challenges we face in our day, the more God pours His strength into our lives as we place our hope in Him and turn to Him for the solutions.*

6. *Some things that could keep a person from depending on Jesus include pride, habitually fantasizing about the life he or she wants instead of the life he or she has, or a belief that Jesus isn't really trustworthy. There are many possibilities!*

7. *It took a great deal of courage for Peter and John to publicly proclaim Jesus as the Messiah, the Jewish King and Savior, to the very people who had rejected Him during His earthly life and had Him put to death. The members of the Sanhedrin were certainly able to throw Peter and John in jail, and they were also able to have them stoned to death for blasphemy. It is likely the Sanhedrin could even have persuaded the Roman governor to crucify these disciples of Jesus for rejecting Caesar as king. Peter and John not only proclaimed their Master's kingship to the Sanhedrin but also refused to stop publicly speaking about Him when the Sanhedrin ordered them to stop.*

8. *Peter and John had seen Jesus risen from the dead, face to face, and had spoken with Him and eaten with Him. They knew beyond a doubt that Jesus was alive and that, therefore, everything He had told them was true. They* *were bubbling over with the amazing truth that they knew with certainty that Jesus was the promised Messiah.*

9. *Peter and John affirmed God's sovereignty over the situation, and then they prayed, "Lord, consider their threats and enable your servants to speak your word with great boldness. Stretch out your hand to heal and perform signs and wonders through the name of your holy servant Jesus" (verses 29–30). Their attitude was zealous and unafraid.*

10. *Peter and John spoke about what they had seen and heard in the flesh; our experience of Jesus is often thin by comparison. We believe, but we also doubt. Often we haven't relied on Him enough to be convinced that He is really alive and with us. Speaking about our experience of Jesus involves the risk that God will put us in a situation that demands great boldness to speak His word . . . and He will want us to speak. Benefits include the blessing of seeing God act through our lives, and the possibility of bringing others to Christ.*

11. *Answers will vary.*

12. *Answers will vary.*

13. *Responses will vary.*

Session 8: Courage to Withstand the Evil One

1. *Answers will vary. While it is frightening and unsettling to read about Satan being depicted in this way, it is important for us to be aware of the enemy's tactics and how he seeks to destroy believers. The truth is that we have a real enemy who works to keep us separated from God.*

2. *Answers will vary. The image of God as the "Lion of Judah" should give us courage when we consider that our heavenly Father is all-powerful as He works on our behalf. The enemy is no match for God; as Paul wrote, "I am convinced that neither death nor life, neither angels nor demons . . . will* *be able to separate us from the love of God that is in Christ Jesus" (Romans 8:38–39).*

3. *Satan has the power to plant thoughts in our minds. He whispers frightening messages to us, and as we mull these over, soon we are genuinely afraid to step out and do the thing God has given us to do. Satan's goal is to stop us from doing God's will by magnifying in our minds the risks of obedience.*

4. *When Satan attempts to attack us with fear, we can boldly pray (preferably aloud) a prayer that affirms our faith. "I trust You, Jesus!" is a simple example. In addition, we can speak or sing praises to Jesus to help us override the lie Satan wants us to believe. If Satan speaks condemnation, we can remember that Scripture says, "There is now no condemnation for those who are in Christ Jesus" (Romans 8:1).*

5. *Satan works hard to distract us from thoughts of Jesus. He tries to implant in our minds thoughts of worry, mistrust of God, pride, selfishness, and other things that are at odds with faith, hope, and love. Satan and Jesus are at war over our thought life, but Jesus is stronger. We only need to choose Him moment by moment.*

6. *We can say a simple prayer such as, "Jesus, help me!" and then let the Lord fight the battle. If we find we are having trouble with worrisome thoughts, we shouldn't try to drive them away on our own. Instead, we need to pray for Jesus' deliverance—and watch as He does His work. Just making the decision to turn our thoughts over to our Savior and King can be a powerful act of warfare against the enemy.*

7. *God's truth equips us as His children to reject lies about our deepest identity or about what is good or bad to do. Righteousness—a right relationship with God, as well as the character that flows from it—equips us to know what is right or wrong. Doing right is literal warfare against the temptations of the enemy. The gospel of peace equips us for warfare because if* *we act as peacemakers rather than as agents of enmity, we are doing the will of God. Faith allows us to access the power of Jesus. Nothing effective can be done against the enemy without faith in Christ. Salvation is what protects us from eternal judgment—if we have it, we belong to Jesus and the enemy cannot touch us. Reminding ourselves of that fact is key to standing firm. The sword of the Spirit, which is the word of God, tells us what is true and protects us against the enemy's lies.*

8. *It's up to God to attack the enemy; our role is often to stand firm against the enemy's attacks. We do this not in our own strength but in the strength of the One who defeated the enemy by dying and rising again. We operate according to His direction as our Commander.*

9. *As believers, we pray "in the Spirit" because it is through the Holy Spirit that we receive answers to prayer and all empowerment from God. We are to pray constantly—at all times and with perseverance. As we pray, we receive power from God that allows us to stand against the enemy. This is what Paul was seeking when he asked the believers in Ephesus to pray for his ministry.*

10. *Answers will vary. The list of armor and weapons in this passage shows us how many resources God has given His people to defend themselves against the enemy's schemes. We are not left defenseless and alone in the fight. For this reason we can be brave, knowing that God has equipped us with His might and that Jesus has already won the ultimate battle.*

11. *Answers will vary.*

12. *Answers will vary.*

13. *Responses will vary.*

Also Available in the
Jesus Calling® Bible Study Series

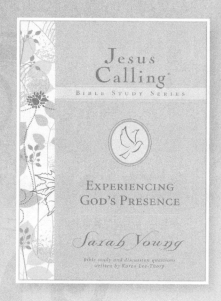

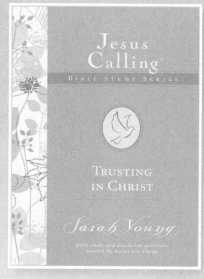

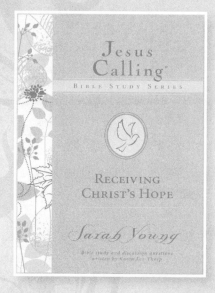

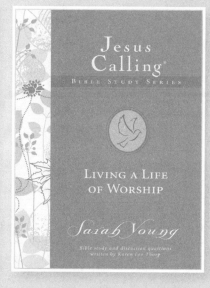

If you liked reading this book, you may enjoy these other titles by *Sarah Young*

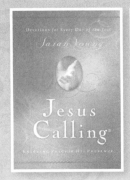

Jesus Calling®
Hardcover

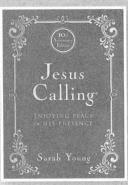

Jesus Calling® 10th Anniversary Edition
Bonded Leather

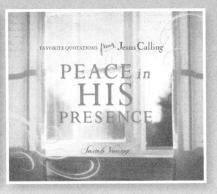

Peace in His Presence:
Favorite Quotations from Jesus Calling®
Padded Hardcover

Jesus Calling® for Kids
Hardcover

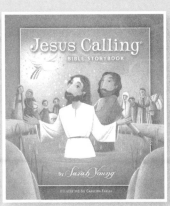

Jesus Calling® Bible Storybook
Hardcover

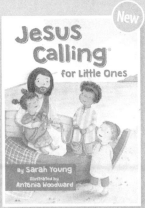

Jesus Calling® for Little Ones
Board Book